P9-CAO-873

Black Hawk

NORTH AMERICAN INDIANS OF ACHIEVEMENT

BLACK HAWK

Sac Rebel

▲▲▲

Nancy Bonvillain

Senior Consulting Editor
W. David Baird
Howard A. White Professor of History
Pepperdine University

HIGHWOOD PUBLIC LIBRARY
102 Highwood Avenue
Highwood, IL 60040-1597
Phone: 432-5404

CHELSEA HOUSE PUBLISHERS

New York   Philadelphia

FRONTISPIECE   Black Hawk, defender of the Sac and Fox homelands, poses together with his emblem, a black sparrow hawk, in an 1832 portrait by George Catlin.

ON THE COVER   This tinted engraving, based on a painting by Charles Bird King, shows Black Hawk as he appeared on his 1833 tour of the eastern United States.

Chelsea House Publishers
EDITORIAL DIRECTOR   Richard Rennert
EXECUTIVE MANAGING EDITOR   Karyn Gullen Browne
COPY CHIEF   Robin James
PICTURE EDITOR   Adrian G. Allen
ART DIRECTOR   Robert Mitchell
MANUFACTURING DIRECTOR   Gerald Levine
PRODUCTION COORDINATOR   Marie Claire Cebrián-Ume

North American Indians of Achievement
SENIOR EDITOR   Marian W. Taylor

Staff for BLACK HAWK
ASSISTANT EDITOR   Margaret Dornfeld
COPY EDITOR   Nicole Greenblatt
EDITORIAL ASSISTANT   Joy Sanchez
SENIOR DESIGNER   Rae Grant
PICTURE RESEARCHER   Lisa Kirchner

Copyright © 1994 by Chelsea House Publishers, a division of Main Line Book Co. All rights reserved.

Printed and bound in Mexico.

3   5   7   9   8   6   4   2

Library of Congress Cataloging-in-Publication Data

Bonvillain, Nancy.
Black Hawk, Sac rebel/Nancy Bonvillain.
    p. cm. — (North American Indians of achievement)
Summary: Discusses the life and times of the Sauk chief who led his people in a struggle to prevent the advance of white settlers in Illinois in the early 1800s.
ISBN 0-7910-1711-7.
ISBN 0-7910-1997-7 (pbk)
1. Black Hawk, Sauk chief, 1767–1838—Juvenile literature. 2. Sauk Indians—Biography—Juvenile literature. 3. Black Hawk War, 1832—Juvenile literature. [1. Black Hawk, Sauk chief, 1767–1838. 2. Sauk Indians—Biography. 3. Indians of North America—Illinois—Biography.] I. Title. II. Title: Black Hawk. III. Series.
E83.83.B6B65 1993   93-19330
973.5'6—dc20   CIP
[B]   AC

CONTENTS

NORTH AMERICAN INDIANS OF ACHIEVEMENT

BLACK HAWK
Sac Rebel

JOSEPH BRANT
Mohawk Chief

BEN NIGHTHORSE CAMPBELL
Cheyenne Chief
and U.S. Legislator

COCHISE
Apache Chief

CRAZY HORSE
Sioux War Chief

CHIEF GALL
Sioux War Chief

GERONIMO
Apache Warrior

HIAWATHA
Founder of the
Iroquois Confederacy

CHIEF JOSEPH
Nez Perce Leader

PETER MACDONALD
Former Chairman of
the Navajo Nation

WILMA MANKILLER
Principal Chief of the Cherokees

OSCEOLA
Seminole Rebel

QUANAH PARKER
Comanche Chief

KING PHILIP
Wampanoag Rebel

POCAHONTAS
Powhatan Peacemaker

PONTIAC
Ottawa Rebel

RED CLOUD
Sioux War Chief

WILL ROGERS
Cherokee Entertainer

SITTING BULL
Chief of the Sioux

TECUMSEH
Shawnee Rebel

JIM THORPE
Sac and Fox Athlete

SARAH WINNEMUCCA
Northern Paiute Writer
and Diplomat

Other titles in preparation

ON INDIAN LEADERSHIP

by W. David Baird
Howard A. White Professor of History
Pepperdine University

Authoritative utterance is in thy mouth, perception is in thy heart, and thy tongue is the shrine of justice," the ancient Egyptians said of their king. From him, the Egyptians expected authority, discretion, and just behavior. Homer's *Iliad* suggests that the Greeks demanded somewhat different qualities from their leaders: justice and judgment, wisdom and counsel, shrewdness and cunning, valor and action. It is not surprising that different people living at different times should seek different qualities from the individuals they looked to for guidance. By and large, a people's requirements for leadership are determined by two factors: their culture and the unique circumstances of the time and place in which they live.

Before the late 15th century, when non-Indians first journeyed to what is now North America, most Indian tribes were not ruled by a single person. Instead, there were village chiefs, clan headmen, peace chiefs, war chiefs, and a host of other types of leaders, each with his or her own specific duties. These influential people not only decided political matters but also helped shape their tribe's social, cultural, and religious life. Usually, Indian leaders held their positions because they had won the respect of their peers. Indeed, if a leader's followers at any time decided that he or she was out of step with the will of the people, they felt free to look to someone else for advice and direction.

Thus, the greatest achievers in traditional Indian communities were men and women of extraordinary talent. They were not only skilled at navigating the deadly waters of tribal politics and cultural customs but also able to, directly or indirectly, make a positive and significant difference in the daily life of their followers.

From the beginning of their interaction with Native Americans, non-Indians failed to understand these features of Indian leadership. Early European explorers and settlers merely assumed that Indians had the same relationship with their leaders as non-Indians had with their kings and queens. European monarchs generally inherited their positions and ruled large nations however they chose, often with little regard for the desires or needs of their subjects. As a result, the settlers of Jamestown saw Pocahontas as a "princess" and Pilgrims dubbed Wampanoag leader Metacom "King Philip," envisioning them in roles very different from those in which their own people placed them.

As more and more non-Indians flocked to North America, the nature of Indian leadership gradually began to change. Influential Indians no longer had to take on the often considerable burden of pleasing only their own people; they also had to develop a strategy of dealing with the non-Indian newcomers. In a rapidly changing world, new types of Indian role models with new ideas and talents continually emerged. Some were warriors; others were peacemakers. Some held political positions within their tribes; others were writers, artists, religious prophets, or athletes. Although the demands of Indian leadership altered from generation to generation, several factors that determined which Indian people became prominent in the centuries after first contact remained the same.

Certain personal characteristics distinguished these Indians of achievement. They were intelligent, imaginative, practical, daring, shrewd, uncompromising, ruthless, and logical. They were constant in friendships, unrelenting in hatreds, affectionate with their relatives, and respectful to their God or gods. Of course, no single Native American leader embodied all these qualities, nor these qualities only. But it was these characteristics that allowed them to succeed.

The special skills and talents that certain Indians possessed also brought them to positions of importance. The life of Hiawatha, the legendary founder of the powerful Iroquois Confederacy, displays the value that oratorical ability had for many Indians in power.

The biography of Cochise, the 19th-century Apache chief, illustrates that leadership often required keen diplomatic skills not only in transactions among tribespeople but also in hardheaded negotiations with non-Indians. For others, such as Mohawk Joseph Brant and Navajo Peter MacDonald, a non-Indian education proved advantageous in their dealings with other peoples.

Sudden changes in circumstance were another crucial factor in determining who became influential in Indian communities. King Philip in the 1670s and Geronimo in the 1880s both came to power when their people were searching for someone to lead them into battle against white frontiersmen who had forced upon them a long series of indignities. Seeing the rising discontent of Indians of many tribes in the 1810s, Tecumseh and his brother, the Shawnee prophet Tenskwatawa, proclaimed a message of cultural revitalization that appealed to thousands. Other Indian achievers recognized cooperation with non-Indians as the most advantageous path during their lifetime. Sarah Winnemucca in the late 19th century bridged the gap of understanding between her people and their non-Indian neighbors through the publication of her autobiography *Life Among the Piutes*. Olympian Jim Thorpe in the early 20th century championed the assimilationist policies of the U.S. government and, with his own successes, demonstrated the accomplishments Indians could make in the non-Indian world. And Wilma Mankiller, principal chief of the Cherokees, continues to fight successfully for the rights of her people through the courts and through negotiation with federal officials.

Leadership among Native Americans, just as among all other peoples, can be understood only in the context of culture and history. But the centuries that Indians have had to cope with invasions of foreigners in their homelands have brought unique hardships and obstacles to the Native American individuals who most influenced and inspired others. Despite these challenges, there has never been a lack of Indian men and women equal to these tasks. With such strong leaders, it is no wonder that Native Americans remain such a vital part of this nation's cultural landscape.

1

"I AM BLACK HAWK"

On June 5, 1831, a delegation of Sac Indian leaders assembled in a council house at Saukenuk, a large Indian village in present-day Illinois. Before them stood General Edmund P. Gaines of the U.S. Army, a man with large ambitions and a quick temper, flanked by a team of officers and a company of armed guards. The two sides had come together to settle ownership rights to Saukenuk—now called Rock Island—and the country around it. The day was hot, and the meeting would be tense—Indians and whites alike felt strongly that their own people were entitled to the fruits of this rich, spacious territory.

The Sacs (also known as Sauks) had lived and farmed on this land for 200 years. Up and down the Mississippi Valley, from Prairie du Chien in the north to the mouth of the Des Moines River in the south, the Sacs and their longstanding allies, the Foxes, had set up thriving communities. A nation of farmers and hunters, the Sac and Fox confederacy had profited both from the region's fertile soil and from its position within the European fur trade, which used the Mississippi River as its main artery. Saukenuk itself was one of the most prosperous Native American villages in the Mississippi Valley. Located on

The war chief Makataimeshekiakiah, or Black Sparrow Hawk, inspired more than 2,000 Sac and Fox Indians to defy the U.S. government and defend their homes along the upper Mississippi River.

a point of land where the Rock River meets the Mississippi, it boasted more than one hundred lodges, built of wooden posts covered with layers of white elm bark. The Sacs who occupied Saukenuk, at one point numbering some 3,000, had enjoyed a life of comfort and plenty. The nearby rapids teemed with fish, and the vast stands of bluegrass on the surrounding prairie provided nourishment for the Indians' horses. Clear, clean water gushed from several springs on a bluff above the village, and in the surrounding countryside grew berries, apples, plums, and nuts. The residents of Saukenuk were able to cultivate several hundred acres of corn, enough to allow a surplus to be sold to white and Indian traders.

For many years, this land had kept the Sac and Fox nation generously fed, clothed, and sheltered. The Indians believed that when they died, their spirits would continue

Indians and whites navigate the waters near an Illinois settlement. Interactions between the Sacs and Foxes and their white neighbors grew more and more tense as the white population expanded. By 1831 settlers had begun to occupy the lodges and fields of Saukenuk.

to dwell among the grasses and waters of the Illinois prairie. The land was their strength and their foundation—they had formed a deep bond with it, and they had no desire to part from it.

The U.S. government had other ideas. For 15 years, government officials claimed, the Sacs and the Foxes had been living on land that no longer belonged to them. According to the whites, the Sacs had sold Saukenuk and the surrounding country to the United States at a council in St. Louis in 1804. Since that time U.S. leaders had allowed the Indians to remain, officials said, only out of their own goodwill. Now settlers needed the land, and it was time for the Indians to leave it. U.S. troops had arrived in Saukenuk. Gaines, their commander, meant to persuade the Sacs and Foxes to give up their villages once and for all and move west, to the far side of the Mississippi River.

The Sacs' war chief, 64-year-old Black Hawk, had arrived for the conference in full battle gear, his skin gleaming with war paint. Like his followers, he came armed; he and his men carried bows and arrows, spears, war clubs, and feathered lances. They presented themselves in this way, Black Hawk said later, "to show the [American] war chief that we were not afraid!"

Indeed, on seeing the Indians thus equipped for battle, some of the officers attending the council recoiled in alarm. Gaines, a tough and experienced Indian fighter and veteran of the War of 1812, remained calm, increased the guard, and ordered his men to remain armed throughout the negotiations. It was his job to move these Indians out of Illinois, and he intended to do exactly that.

Opening the meeting, Gaines reminded Black Hawk sharply that five Indian leaders had made their mark on the Treaty of 1804, which ceded Saukenuk and much more to the U.S. government. In 1816 Black Hawk

General Edmund P. Gaines, who in earlier times had led campaigns against the Creek and the Seminole Indians, confronted Black Hawk and his followers in 1831. Though personally opposed to the government's removal policy, Gaines defended it loyally, convinced that the Sacs would yield in the presence of U.S. troops.

himself, the general emphasized, had signed an additional treaty confirming the agreement. With these documents, according to the United States, the Sacs and the Foxes had given up their right to all their lands east of the Mississippi and part of their hunting grounds west of the great river. Included in the land package were all of the present state of Illinois north of the Illinois River and huge sections of modern Wisconsin and Missouri. For these 50 million acres, the new U.S. government had paid the Sac and Fox Indians $2,234 and promised to give them $1,000 worth of goods each year.

Black Hawk, who had long served as the Sacs' most strident voice of resistance, had been over this ground many times before. Some days earlier, when he had received word that a "great war chief" (Gaines) was on his way to Rock River with a large company of soldiers, he consulted a friend from the Winnebago tribe known for his powers of prophecy. When Black Hawk asked how he should proceed, the prophet told him that a dream had revealed to him the meaning of the war chief's visit. "The object of his mission was to frighten us from our village, that the white people might get our land for nothing," Black Hawk learned from his friend. The prophet assured him further that the army "dare not, and would, not hurt any of us. . . . All we had to do to retain our village, was to refuse any, and every offer that might be made by this war chief."

Now, finding himself face to face with Gaines, Black Hawk spoke with cool determination. In 1816, when he had "touched the goose quill to the treaty" (made his mark with a goose-quill pen), he was agreeing to let the whites hunt on tribal land, no more, the war chief said. This land had been home to Sacs and Foxes for generations, and they would not leave it. Meeting the general's eyes, the Sac leader declared that his people had a right to live in the land where their ancestors had farmed, hunted, and built their villages. As he spoke, Black Hawk said later, he felt a wave of indignation rise within him, but he made an effort to conceal his anger, and his words were slow and quiet.

Gaines, who could see that the Sac chief had many supporters among his delegation, also struggled to keep his temper. Tight-lipped but still civil, he addressed the Indians:

> The president [Andrew Jackson] is very sorry to be put to the trouble and expense of sending a large body of soldiers here, to remove you from the lands you have long since ceded to the United States. Your Great Father has already warned you repeatedly to leave the country; and he is very sorry to find that you have disobeyed his orders. Your Great Father wishes you well; and asks nothing from you but what is reasonable and right. I hope you will consult your own interest, and leave the country you are occupying, and go to the other side of the Mississippi.

Enraged, the chiefs and warriors in Black Hawk's company rose to challenge the general's counsel. The Indian leaders shouted that they stood behind the words of their war chief and would continue to do so—they would remain at Saukenuk until the end, and when they died, "lay their bones with those of their ancestors."

Finally Black Hawk himself—who had momentarily withdrawn from the discussion, his blanket wrapped around him—leapt to his feet in fury. "We have never sold our country," he said. "We never received any money or goods from the American father! And we are determined to hold on to our village!"

At this show of resistance Gaines's anger flared. He was not there for a debate, he snapped, but to see that the Indians kept their word. Their choice was not whether to leave the land or stay on it, but whether to leave peacefully or at the point of a bayonet. His voice rising,

he told the Sacs to stop listening to their old leader. "Who is Black Hawk?" he shouted. "Who is Black Hawk?"

Drawing himself to his full height, Black Hawk responded in a measured tone. "You have asked who is Black Hawk? I am a Sac. My forefather was a *Sac*. And all the nations call me a SAC!"

By now, all evidence of Gaines's courteous restraint had evaporated. "My business is to remove you, peaceably if I can, but forcibly if I must," he said, his voice rising as he went on. "I will now give you two days to remove in—and if you do not cross the Mississippi within that time, I will adopt measures to force you away!"

Despite Gaines's determined stance, it would prove no simple matter to force Black Hawk to obey American law. And despite Black Hawk's unshakable conviction in the justice of his cause, persuading the U.S. government to see it his way presented an equally daunting task.

To add to Black Hawk's troubles, the Sac and Fox nation, at one time a powerful and prosperous union, was now divided into factions. Though Black Hawk commanded a loyal following, another segment of the Sacs, led by the war chief's rival—the young and eloquent Keokuk—refused to support him, content to comply with the government's every demand. Forced to combat the white forces without the full support of his people, Black Hawk knew he faced an enormous challenge, but he did not waver. His spirit was steeled for battle.

The Swimmer, portrayed in 1832 by George Catlin, was one of Black Hawk's loyal followers. By the time Black Hawk met with Gaines, many Sac and Fox warriors had defected to the camp of the old war chief's rival, Keokuk.

2

GROWING UP SAC

This 19th-century drawing by Swiss historian Carl Bodmer shows a pair of Sac warriors in traditional dress.

Black Hawk was born in 1767 in Saukenuk, the largest village of the Sac and Fox Indian nation. Situated on the east side of the Mississippi River, where present-day Illinois borders Iowa, the village was, according to one witness, "the wonder of all who visited it."

Like other Sac communities, Saukenuk consisted of rows of summer lodges made from wooden frames covered with white elm bark, each building home to one or several families. Averaging 40 to 60 feet long and about 20 feet wide, the lodges contained long benches covered with blankets and skins, and an open area in the center where the Indians built fires and prepared their food. Fences, built of poles with melon vines winding along them, surrounded some of the homes in Saukenuk. In addition to the large fields of corn spreading out around the village, the women of each family tended gardens near their homes, raising pumpkins, beans, and squash.

An English traveler visiting the village the year before Black Hawk's birth described it as "the largest and best built Indian town" with "regular and spacious streets." It was in these affluent, orderly surroundings that Black Hawk came into the world and spent his childhood.

Much of what history knows about Black Hawk comes from his autobiography, which he dictated to an interpreter when he was 66 years old. This narrative reveals little about the Sac leader's early life, but very likely it followed a path similar to that of other Sac children.

Sac families generally celebrated the birth of a child by sponsoring a public feast. Black Hawk's father, descended from a line of chiefs, no doubt entertained his guests lavishly in honor of his newborn son. The entire village was invited on such occasions, and everyone shared in the food, dancing, and exchange of gifts.

Festivities of this kind were common among the Sacs, whose culture emphasized cooperation and generosity, and whose environment supported them amply. The Indians fed on fish from the Rock and Mississippi rivers; game, fruit, and nuts from the Illinois woods; and corn, beans, and squash from the farms near their villages. Black Hawk recalled: "We always had plenty. Our children never cried with hunger, nor our people were never in want." Amid this bounty, the Sacs were able to devote much of their time to their families and friends, and the younger members of the tribe enjoyed a great deal of love and attention.

In the summers, Black Hawk's family probably lived together in the lodge belonging to his father's relatives. Though the building was shared by several families, each family had their own living quarters within it. The lodge where Black Hawk grew up may have originally been the home of his grandfather on his father's side. Usually, the sons of a given Sac family continued to live in the same lodge as their parents even after they married. Their wives came to live with them in that lodge, and there they would raise their children. A daughter in a Sac family would live in her parents' home until marriage, when she would move into the house of her husband and his family. Fathers and their sons, then—or groups of

Commenting on the Sac and Fox begging dance, pictured here, Catlin wrote that the Indians performed it "singing a song of importunity, and extending their hands for presents, which they allege are to gladden the hearts of the poor, and ensure a blessing to the giver."

brothers—typically formed the basis of Sac households. A lodge often contained elder parents, their sons and sons' families, and the elder couple's unmarried daughters.

In Sac society, women and men played separate roles, each of which contributed significantly to the support of the family and the tribe as a whole. In the summer, women spent most of their days in the fields, tilling the soil, planting, tending, and harvesting huge crops of corn, and sometimes cultivating smaller plots of other vegetables. Those with small children took their babies with them when they went to work. Tucked into a blanket and strapped to a cradle board, even the youngest infants could travel on their mothers' backs out into the cornfields. Older children would help the women as they worked. When the women went out to gather wild fruits, herbs, and nuts, or to fish in the nearby streams, their children again accompanied them. Women and children would also collect the bark and reeds from which the

Indians wove the mats that made up their winter lodges. Black Hawk, like other Sacs, probably spent most of his early childhood out of doors, at his mother's side.

While the women in the Sac tribe farmed, brought in what goods they found in nature, and cared for the children, the men fished in the streams and rivers and hunted deer, elk, and buffalo on the great midwestern prairie. Along the banks of the Rock and the Mississippi, Sac men also sought out such smaller game as muskrat, raccoon, beaver, and rabbit. The Sacs hunted not only for food, but for furs to sell to neighboring tribes and to the white traders who frequented Saukenuk. When they were not hunting, the men were often negotiating with their partners in trade, usually in order to obtain tools, weapons, and other goods made of metal, which in Black Hawk's time only white people could supply. Sometimes the men paid for these goods with some of the corn that the women had harvested, with beeswax gathered by women and men, or with lead that members of the tribe had mined from a region to the north of Saukenuk.

As Black Hawk grew older, the men in his family began to teach him the skills he would need when he reached adulthood. The tribe held competitive games during the summer months, and these were part of a young boy's training. The best known of the games, a forerunner of modern lacrosse, was played on a field as long as 300 yards, with goalposts erected at either end. Armed with long-handled wooden rackets, hundreds of players fought violently to send a small deerskin ball across the goal of their opponents. The Sacs also raced horses, and to win such a sporting event was a matter of great prestige for a young Indian. Spectators and even the participants themselves placed bets as a part of their summer activities, wagering guns, horses, blankets, and other possessions on the outcome of the games and races.

In general, summer was a time of feasting and

celebrating in the Sac community. After a hunt, the Indians might indulge for several days in bouts of eating, dancing, and game playing, sometimes making themselves ill in their enthusiasm. The Sacs also used this time of plenty to visit their relatives and friends and renew social bonds. It was during this season that young people got to know one another and sometimes decided on a future marriage.

As the summer drew to a close, when the crops had been brought in, the Sacs began preparations for the move to their winter quarters, the location of which shifted throughout the season, depending on where game could be found. A tribal council convened to assign hunting areas to separate groups of families and to decide when the tribe would leave their summer settlement. A crier then made the rounds of the village, announcing the date of departure. Before leaving, the Indians stored dried corn, beans, and berries in their lodges and in containers buried in the ground so that when they returned the following spring they would have a supply of food ready to eat.

On the appointed day, the Sacs split up into smaller groups, usually of brothers and their wives and children, and set out for their winter hunting grounds. Older members of the family and women and children traveled by canoe while the men followed on horseback. Arriving in their allotted area, the Indians set up temporary camps, constructing simple dwellings of bark, branches, and earth. If the hunting in this region was good, the group might stay at the same camp for an entire season. If not, they eventually moved elsewhere and hoped for better results. When the period of severe cold arrived, the men limited their activities to the occasional hunting and trapping of muskrat and beaver, which could always be found along the rivers and streams of Sac territory. For the rest of the time, they waited out the winter inside their winter lodges in front of a warm fire.

When spring approached, the hunting and trapping expeditions would revive for a time. Then the various groups of Sacs would reassemble at a designated spot along the Mississippi and return together to their permanent home. Living for a while off the caches of food they had left behind the previous autumn, the Sacs would repair any damage to their homes caused by deterioration or bad weather, then prepare once more for the planting season. Traveling with his family this way from year to year, Black Hawk gradually came to know every hill and valley of the Sacs' vast homelands.

In addition to the cycle of seasonal migration, religious events marked the passing of the year. On returning to their villages in the spring, the Sacs would hold a burial ceremony, known as the medicine feast, for those who

Indians hunt deer by torchlight. Such game as deer, elk, beaver, and muskrat flourished along the streams and rivers of Sac and Fox territory.

had died during the year. Having purchased valuable goods from the white traders with the pelts they had obtained over the winter, the relatives of the deceased would distribute them to their friends, according to Black Hawk, "to show the Great Spirit that they are humble, so that he will take pity on them." Later, when the corn had been planted, the men and women of each Sac village would come together for a festival called the crane dance, which lasted for two or three days. This ritual was followed by a second dance in honor of the tribe's warriors, after which individual lodges would take turns hosting feasts in praise of the Great Spirit. Toward the end of the summer, when the corn became ripe, at a given signal the children of the village pulled ears for roasting, and the Sacs would feast again as a gesture of thanksgiving.

The Sacs believed not only in the divine power they called the Great Spirit but also in individual spirits that lived in the world around them and had a direct influence on their lives. A spirit might serve as the guardian of a specific place in nature, such as a mountain, a river, or a cave. When a Sac Indian approached one of these places, he or she would thank the spirit there for its protection. Individuals could also appeal to the spirit world for a personal guardian. On reaching adulthood, a young Sac could begin to pray for the aid of a spirit protector. If such prayers were heard, a spirit would give the seeker a sign of its presence, usually in the form of an object such as an animal's tooth, a feather, or a stone of unusual appearance. The recipient would keep the object as a token of the spirit protector, and pray to it in times of distress, after which the spirit might respond with a comforting message or instruction.

The Sacs believed that spirits could also appear to people in visions and dreams. If someone was troubled

by illness or misfortune, a spirit might offer a cure or solution. Likewise, when someone had to make an important decision, a spirit might appear and advise that person on the proper course of action. Early in his life, Black Hawk had a vision in which a black sparrow hawk revealed itself as his personal protector. It was from this sign that the aspiring warrior took his adult name.

Sac religious life involved a deep appreciation of family history and a sense of enduring communion with departed members of the tribe. Every Sac Indian belonged not only to his or her immediate family but also to a clan, a group of people who considered themselves related through descent from a common ancestor. The Sac groups included the Bear, Wolf, Bass, and Thunder clans, as well as eight others, each one named after an animal or a natural element. Sac children always belonged to the same clan as their father. When they grew up, they had

Sac and Fox men, wearing paint and bearing weapons, participate in a war dance. Warfare played an important role in Sac and Fox culture; warriors who showed courage and skill in battle increased their influence within the tribe.

to marry someone from a different clan. Because wives and husbands had to belong to different clans, children could never belong to the same clan as their mother.

Each clan kept a collection of sacred possessions stored in a special bundle known as a medicine bag. These objects were usually tokens of good fortune taken from nature, such as animal claws, teeth, or eagle feathers. Powerful medicines also went into the clan's sacred bundle. Twice a year, each clan held a ceremony in which the Indians paid homage to the magic of the medicine bag.

In addition to their religious function, the clans played an important role in the tribe's system of government. Like many Native American tribes, the Sacs had one set of leaders that advised the community on civil issues, and another set for guidance in matters of war. The peace chiefs, as the first set were often called, each represented a different clan. They generally inherited their position, but the degree of power they exercised depended on their own personality and behavior. To win the support of his people, a peace chief needed to be intelligent, generous, kind, and good tempered. It was his job to be fair in his judgments and helpful to others.

Of the peace chiefs, the Sacs recognized one man as the head. This chief, chosen from the Sturgeon clan, enjoyed a special status in the tribe but, like the other leaders, could not force anyone to comply with his decisions—all the members of the Sac tribe had the right to make up their own minds and do what they thought best.

When important problems arose in the community, the peace chiefs met in council to discuss them and suggest solutions. Tribe members with an unresolved dispute might take the case to the council and ask for advice. If the Sacs were negotiating an alliance or treaty with another group, the council deliberated over the

Sac warriors made ample use of the metal goods they acquired from European traders. This Indian holds a war club equipped with a steel blade and studded with brass nails.

proposed agreement together, each leader offering his opinion. When the council reached a decision, the chiefs chose one man to carry the message to the rest of the tribe. The crier, as he was called, would travel to each Sac settlement and publicly announce the outcome of the meeting. The council might also send out a crier if the Sacs needed to communicate with individuals representing them abroad.

A second division of leaders, known to white observers as war chiefs, would organize and lead attacks on foreign tribes and, when their settlements were threatened by an enemy, plan the Sacs' defense. Two men, selected for their courage and success in battle, held this position. They retained their title as long as their reputation as a great warrior lasted. Like the peace chiefs, war chiefs could not force anyone to follow their plans, and other men could also lead war parties, as long as they were able to attract a sufficient following. The structure of Sac armies was always loose: if a warrior approved of a leader's plans and aims, he went along—if not, he stayed home and attended to his other duties.

Though Black Hawk claimed hereditary rights to the rank of civil chief, it was as a war chief that he would rise to prominence.

HIGHWOOD PUBLIC LIBRARY

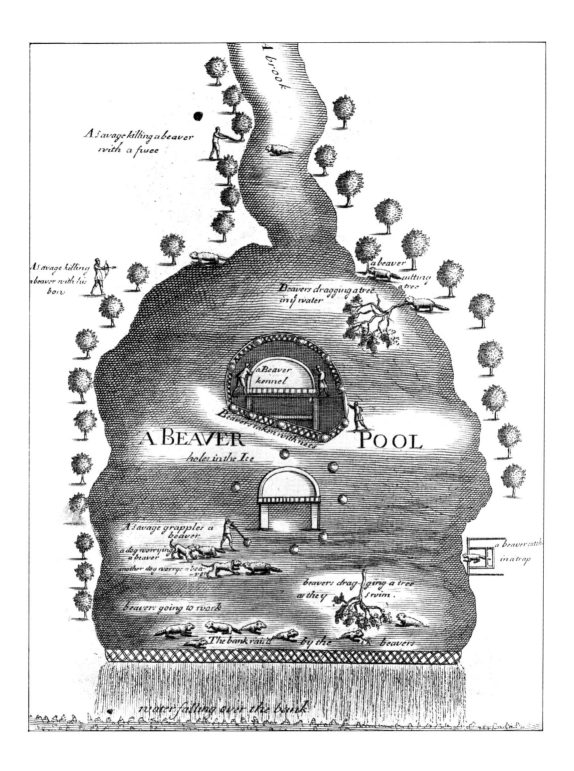

3

A WAR CHIEF
COMES OF AGE

In 1767, the year of Black Hawk's birth, the Sacs were still relative newcomers to the Mississippi Valley. Black Hawk's grandfather had come from northern Wisconsin; before that, if family legend is to be believed, the tribe may have lived as far east as Montreal, Canada. It was over a period of many decades that the Sac Indians, driven by a combination of influences, moved west and finally south to their luxuriant lands along the Rock River.

During the 16th and 17th centuries, not only the Sacs, but Indian tribes throughout North America faced a period of enormous upheaval. At the root of this shift was the advance of the Europeans, who, following the arrival in the New World of the Italian explorer Christopher Columbus in 1492, came to the American continent in ever increasing numbers in search of wealth and property.

For the Indians of the Northeast, one of the most important effects of the European presence was a change in intertribal relations resulting from the Indians' involvement in the fur trade. The Iroquois, a powerful Indian confederacy based in the area that is now New York State, were some of the Europeans' earliest partners

This 18th-century diagram provides an overview of European knowledge about the beaver: its natural environment, its habits, and the methods Indians used to hunt it. As products made from beaver and other animal pelts increased in popularity, Indians across the continent became more deeply involved in the fur trade, a development that changed their lives forever.

in trade, and they quickly began to depend on the goods the whites offered them. Determined to protect their interests, the Iroquois fought to maintain control of trade relations between whites and Indians. To eliminate competition, or to coerce other tribes into trading only through them, they often resorted to violence.

The Iroquois's actions prompted retaliation, the conflicts grew more frequent, and soon Indians throughout the Northeast found themselves caught in a web of near constant warfare. The turmoil drove many tribes to abandon their homes for lands further west. These migrations, unfortunately, caused further conflict—most of the western lands were occupied by Indians already, and these groups, if they were unable to defend their territory, in turn felt compelled to leave. The Sacs, threatened both by Iroquois warriors—ranging far north and west of their own lands—and by other tribes who had fled the Iroquois, were among the Native American tribes caught up in this ill-fated sequence of events.

Sandstone cliffs shelter an Indian village on Mackinack Island, Michigan. The Sacs lived in this region, near Michigan's upper peninsula, until the 17th century, when conflicts with other tribes drove them southwest toward what is now Wisconsin.

Though they may once have occupied regions farther east, the earliest historical records place the Sacs—whose name in their own language, *Osakiwug*, means "people of the yellow earth"—in the upper peninsula of present-day Michigan. Sometime in the first half of the 17th century, pressured by intertribal warfare, the Sacs left this home and traveled west into northern Wisconsin. Finding the land suitable for farming, they set up villages around Green Bay and soon became friendly with most of their Indian neighbors: the Kickapoo, Potawatomi, Fox, Winnebago, Menominee, Miami, and Illinois tribes. The Sacs had much in common with these tribes—they spoke languages that were very similar (all belonging to what linguists call the Algonquian family of languages), they practiced many of the same rituals, and they all supported themselves through a combination of farming and hunting.

Near their home at Green Bay, the Sacs also encountered French explorers, traders, and missionaries. In 1667,

Competing tribes wage war on Lake Superior. During the 1600s, intertribal disputes over territorial and trading rights inspired many such battles.

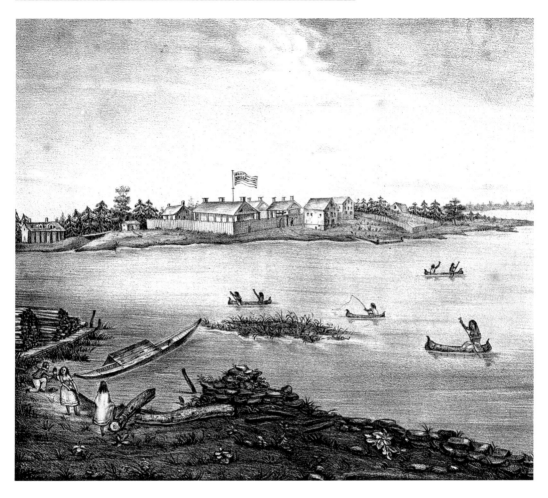

French traders at Chequamegon, a popular trading post on the southern shore of Lake Superior, recorded a number of visits from members of the Sac tribe. Traveling around Green Bay, a French Jesuit of the same period wrote that the Sac Indians in that region were "very numerous." Throughout the late 1600s and on into the following century, the Sacs maintained friendly relations with French traders in the Great Lakes region. They quickly established themselves as partners in trade, offering the white men animal skins—especially beaver, deer, and muskrat—and receiving in return such metal

Indians and whites share the natural resources of Green Bay, Wisconsin, around 1840. From the early 1600s to the middle of the next century, the Sacs made their homes along Green Bay.

objects as guns, nails, knives, axes, and pots. As it had with the Iroquois, such traffic with white traders would eventually become a crucial element of Sac life.

It was also during this period that the Sacs joined forces with the Fox tribe, developing an alliance so strong that from the late 18th century on, white officials would treat the two tribes as a single nation. The Foxes, who lived near the shores of Lake Superior, shared many of the Sacs' customs, and the two tribes communicated easily with one another. Being fewer in number, the Foxes began to look to the more powerful Sacs for protection, and for a time, the Sacs helped to mediate between the Foxes and French traders. In the early 18th century, when a dispute erupted between the Foxes and the French, the Sacs, though professing neutrality, in fact helped their Indian neighbors evict the white man from their lands. Finally, in 1733, the French launched a full-scale assault on the Foxes, and many of them took refuge among the Sacs. The Sacs refused to deliver the fugitives over to their enemies, and the French promptly attacked both parties. Although the Indians beat back their assailants, they eventually decided to abandon the region and together headed south into present-day Iowa and Illinois.

The French traders' dealings with the Indians had been profitable, and in time their relations with the Sac and Fox nation improved. Responding to traders' appeals, some Sacs returned to Wisconsin and continued to live there for a number of years. By the late 1760s, however, they had left the region once more to be with the rest of the tribe. The Sacs, at this point, had founded Saukenuk and several smaller villages along the Rock River and the Mississippi—putting down roots just south of the Foxes, who had settled around the lower Wisconsin River.

The Sacs and the Foxes found prosperity in their adopted home, but they did not find peace. As with other groups of Indians whose circumstances caused them to relocate, the Sacs who came to live on the prairies of Illinois and Iowa did so at the expense of other Indian tribes. Displacing the Osage and the Illinois Indians, the Sacs soon made enemies not only of these tribes but also of the Cherokees and the Chippewas, though they maintained their friendly relations with the Potawatomis and Winnebagos to the north. The alliances and hostilities that developed during these early years of the Sacs' life in the Mississippi Valley would time and again leave their mark on Black Hawk's career, both as a warrior and as a spokesman for the Sac and Fox nation.

Meanwhile, even as their commerce with the French continued, the Sacs found that in their new surroundings they could also trade with the British and the Spanish, both of whom had set up trading posts along the Mississippi River and established a thriving business with the Indians of that region. By the time Black Hawk was in his early youth, the ambitions of the Sac and Fox nation had already risen dramatically; eager for the Europeans' alcohol, tools, weapons, and other manufactured goods, the men of both tribes hunted and trapped with ever-increasing zeal. During their long winter expeditions, the Indians kept their traders informed of their whereabouts, and the traders would often trail them and set up shop alongside their temporary encampments. Bands of Sacs and Foxes would make frequent trips to British posts along the Great Lakes and to the Spanish at St. Louis, where officials offered them gifts and entertainment.

By 1775, the Sacs and Foxes had found a further trade incentive: at their posts on the lower Mississippi, the Spanish dealt not only in manufactured goods but also in horses. Once within reach of a steady supply of these animals, the Indians' lives changed immeasurably. Sac hunters on horseback were able to travel much longer distances than they could ever have gone on foot. Horses also helped the Indians carry hides and meat from their hunting sites to trading posts and back to their villages. As the Sacs and Foxes began to travel farther and haul back heavier loads, their hunting expeditions became more lucrative.

Still a young boy during these years of change, training for a life of hunting and warfare, Black Hawk could hardly have been aware of the many risks and opportunities expanding before him, but his aspirations were high. The young Sac, standing in awe before Saukenuk's warriors—who would boast of their feats in the village square on their day of honor—awaited impatiently the day when he too would be allowed to wear paint and feathers.

Though he would make his living through hunting and trade, Black Hawk hoped above all to distinguish himself in battle. The Sacs had long conferred power and prestige on their war heroes, and some of the boy's early experiences may have convinced him even further of the value of success in warfare.

Approaching adulthood at the outbreak of the American Revolution, Black Hawk was to witness chaos and bloodshed even before he first entered battle. Like many Indian tribes, the Sacs, who had developed no firm loyalties with either the British or their colonists when the Americans declared their independence, nevertheless became caught up in the conflict between them.

As hostilities between British and American troops spread westward, both sides began to petition the Sacs for aid. By this time the Sacs had interacted with American as well as British traders and could not agree on which party to support. Those Sacs who had good relations with American traders—dealers who had no permanent posts

Osage warriors stand ready for battle. Black Hawk's early campaigns against the Osages brought him a reputation for courage and ability in warfare.

near the Sacs but often traveled through their lands—favored the American side. Those Sacs who had developed partnerships with the British had no wish to break these ties, and they argued for aid to the British.

The British had another argument in their favor: they promised to protect Sac territory from the intrusion of American settlers. By the time of the revolutionary war, westbound white families had begun to infiltrate the Sacs' hunting lands. The Sacs were unhappy with the situation, and many of them hoped the British army would change it.

The Sacs failed to unite on behalf of either side, and few of their warriors ever entered the conflict. Nevertheless, in 1780, American troops attacked them. The marauding American soldiers burned some of the largest Sac villages—those that lay along the Rock River—and killed many of the Sacs who lived there, destroying their farms and forcing the survivors to flee for safety. Not only were these raids unprovoked, but the Sacs at Rock River had actually been on the side that supported the Americans. In reaction to the attacks, the Sacs came together and threw their support to the British. Sac leaders would one day refer to the episode as proof of the Americans' treachery.

As the war drew to a close, Black Hawk came of age as a Sac warrior. When he was 15, he began to take part in raids against the Osages, who lived along the Missouri River, and whose hostility toward the Sacs was by this time well established. During one of his first actions, he won honors for wounding an enemy. Later, the young warrior joined his father in a more ambitious assault on the Osages and quickly proved his valor. "Standing by my father's side, I saw him kill his antagonist, and tear the scalp from his head," Black Hawk recalled in his autobiography. "I rushed furiously upon another, smote him to the earth with my tomahawk—run my lance through his body—took off his scalp, and returned in triumph to my father!" Black Hawk's achievement filled him with pride. With it, he had earned the right to join his fellow warriors in their victory celebration, the scalp dance.

Black Hawk's career progressed rapidly. Within a few months, having demonstrated both skill and bravery, he was leading his own expeditions against the Osages—first a party of 7, and soon after that an army of 180. Before departing on these campaigns, the young Sac would devote himself to a session of praying and fasting. Sometimes the Great Spirit would reveal to him the location of an enemy, offer him an omen of victory, or help rally more warriors to his side. Sac war parties could not always be persuaded to follow through with a mission when the odds of attaining glory seemed small. Black Hawk himself, however, once on the warpath, remained determined "never to return without some trophy of victory."

After an unsuccessful raid during his first year at war, Black Hawk went for some time without a sufficient following to wage war again, and in the interim the Osages attacked the Sacs repeatedly. Finally, at the age of 19, he recruited a party of 200, marched out against the Osages, and beat them soundly, discouraging them from further aggression.

The Osages having retreated, the Sacs turned their attention toward the Cherokees, an enemy of long standing. Hearing of a Cherokee band that had murdered a group of Sac women and children, Black Hawk's father resolved to lead a small party of Sacs against them, and the young warrior joined him. The expedition proved fateful. Near the Meramec River, south of St. Louis, the Sacs met a large force of Cherokees, and in the ensuing battle Black Hawk's father was killed. Distressed at his loss, Black Hawk nevertheless took command and swiftly drove back the powerful Cherokees.

When the battle was over, Black Hawk returned to his father's side. Sadly, he removed the old warrior's medicine bag and fastened it to his own clothing. This sacred bundle—containing cedar leaves, a buffalo tail, and the skin of a hawk—had been passed down from father to son for generations. Black Hawk then buried his father and the other warriors who had died in the conflict.

Black Hawk mourned his father for the next five years, blackening his face and regularly fasting and praying to the Great Spirit. He did not engage in warfare during this time but attended to his civil duties, hunting and fishing with the rest of the tribe.

When the mourning period was over, Black Hawk, eager to revenge his father's death, set out to battle anew. In his absence from the battlefield, the Osages had begun to threaten the Sacs' security once again, and the young war leader, hoping to destroy their power once and for all, now assaulted them with a force of 500 Sacs and Foxes and 100 Iowas. The enemy was quickly subdued. Black Hawk then recruited another war party and traveled to the country of the Cherokees, but the band succeeded only in capturing five members of the tribe. Deep as his hatred was, Black Hawk could not find it in himself to kill so small a party, and he soon released them.

Finally, Black Hawk led a large party against the Osages and two Illinois tribes, the Chippewas and the Kaskaskias, beginning an extensive and exhausting campaign that would continue until he reached the age of 35. By the close of the 18th century, the Sacs had driven most of their Indian enemies from their territory. Resuming their rounds of planting, harvesting, hunting, trading, and feasting, they began to reap the fruits of peace and security. Black Hawk took a wife—an attractive, hard-working woman named Asshewequa, or Singing Bird—and the two began to raise a family. But the Sacs' quiet life was not to last. America, now free of its ties to Britain, was moving westward, and more and more a new enemy—the white settler—was encroaching on Indian lands.

4

THE CRISIS BEGINS

When the long conflict with their Indian rivals was over, Black Hawk and other Sac hunters promptly returned to their main objective of accumulating wealth through trade. Their first peacetime winter hunt rewarded them well, inspiring them to make the trip to St. Louis; there, to their satisfaction, their "Spanish father" welcomed them with open arms. The Sacs had generally enjoyed good relations with the Spanish in the past, and on this occasion the trading post official showered them with presents and invited them to dance and celebrate throughout the town.

Their next visit proved less auspicious. Arriving at St. Louis in the spring of 1804, Black Hawk observed that the town had changed. "I discovered," he wrote, "that all was not right: every countenance seemed sad and gloomy! I inquired the cause, and was informed that the Americans were coming to take possession of the town and country."

Indeed, the United States had been moving toward occupation of the Mississippi Valley for some time. As early as 1800, the U.S. Congress had set up a government for the nation's holdings to the west of Ohio. Indiana Territory, as the region was named, stretched from the Ohio River to the southern border of Canada and west to

This unusual portrait of Black Hawk, painted by an unknown artist, shows the war chief wearing a European shirt and a crownlike headdress. As their commerce with white traders and government officials continued, the Sacs and Foxes, like other Indian nations, began to make European tools and clothing a part of their own culture.

43

William Henry Harrison, who had served in the military during a series of U.S.–Indian conflicts in the 1790s, became governor of Indiana Territory in 1800. He negotiated numerous treaties for the purchase of Indian lands.

the Mississippi. William Henry Harrison, a military man who had been active in the affairs of the nation's western frontier for many years, became the region's governor. His constituents included some 5,500 settlers. Valuable as recognition of the territory may have been to these settlers, it boded ill for the many thousands of Native Americans—among them more than 4,000 Sacs—who also lived in the region.

Yet American settlement was to spread still further. In 1803, President Thomas Jefferson acquired a vast tract of land spreading north from the Gulf of Mexico to Canada and west from the Mississippi River to the Rocky Mountains. This area, known as the Louisiana Purchase, had originally belonged to the French, who ceded it to Spain in 1762—shortly before Black Hawk came to know the region. In 1800, it had quietly been transferred back to France, but the Sacs would have seen few signs of the transaction—Napoleon, the leader of the French at that time, ceded the area without ever occupying it.

It was with the sale of this land, then, that the Sacs were to lose their Spanish partners in trade—who, according to Black Hawk, "appeared to us like brothers"—in exchange for U.S. government officials. Shortly after Black Hawk received news of their approach, a detachment of U.S. soldiers took formal possession of St. Louis.

The Sacs were dismayed. Up until this point, the tribe had been able to keep their contact with the new nation to a minimum. Since the United States was formed, American traders had begun to travel down the Ohio River toward the Indians' home, and some Sac hunters had begun to do business with them. For the most part, however, the Sacs had remained loyal to their British associates—who had kept posts around the Great Lakes and still circulated through Sac country—and their Spanish friends at St. Louis. Both of these parties, recognizing in the American presence a threat to their

Settlers build a village on the western frontier. With the purchase of Louisiana Territory in 1803, the government sought to open up vast stretches of prairie land to white settlers.

livelihood, had advised the Indians not to trust the newcomers. From their Indian allies, the Sacs had heard nothing but bad accounts of the Americans, and their own experience during the revolutionary war had taught them to be wary.

The Indians' caution was well advised—having acquired Louisiana, one of Jefferson's first aims was to obtain title to the lands held by the Indians who lived there and officially open the territory to white settlement. The Sacs' fertile hunting grounds, which spanned the border between the Indiana and Louisiana territories, were prime country, and the president assigned Governor Harrison the task of negotiating an agreement with the tribe.

Harrison, having set up his government at Vincennes on the Wabash River, had already made gestures in this direction. In 1802, the governor had invited the Sacs and Foxes, along with several other tribes whose lands lay in Indiana Territory, to a meeting at Vincennes, where he planned to negotiate permanent boundaries between them and the United States. To Harrison's annoyance, the Sacs did not attend, and relations between the Indians and white settlers—who were infiltrating Sac lands in increasing numbers—remained uneasy for two more years.

By 1804, the Sacs had begun to grow uncomfortable about their nebulous position with respect to the United States, and a number of them expressed their eagerness to come to terms. Many Sacs felt that their old rivals the Osages, who had worked out an agreement with the new white power, enjoyed special privileges under U.S. protection, and the Sacs sought to receive the same treatment. Others, however, angered by the settlers' disregard for their authority, believed that the whites' respect could only be won through intimidation.

Tensions soon erupted in violence. A party of Sacs attacked a white settlement on the Cuivre River, a few miles north of St. Louis, and officials arriving on the scene reported finding "three persons murdered in a most barbarous manner, with their scalps taken off." All around St. Louis, settlers flew into a panic. Those who remained at the Cuivre River withdrew behind a half-built stockade and sent an urgent request to St. Louis for arms, ammunition, and reinforcements. Rumors spread that the Sacs were stirring up antiwhite feelings among the Potawatomis and, in their disdain for the U.S. government, were dragging American flags from the tails of their horses. Outraged, some settlers wanted to mount an immediate attack on the Sac villages nearest St. Louis, and the army commander dissuaded them only "with difficulty, and upon promises of ample justice." The Indians themselves feared retaliation, and many fled their homes.

Major James Bruff, the commander at St. Louis, sent a message to the Sacs demanding that they surrender the warriors who had committed the murders on the Cuivre. "There is but one opinion here," he told his superior officer. "Unless those Murderers are demanded; given up and examples made of them; our Frontier will be continually harassed by Murders and Robberies."

Meanwhile, Harrison had come to St. Louis to organize the administration of the Louisiana district. Recognizing an opportunity, he ordered the St. Louis Indian agent to summon the Sac and Fox chiefs to a council, promising them they would be treated "as friends and allies of the United States." The Sacs responded promptly. Five chiefs traveled to St. Louis, bringing with them, as their tribal council had agreed, one of the men who had been involved in the Cuivre River incident. After surrendering the warrior, the Sac leaders hoped to win his pardon by offering goods to the families of those who had been killed—to "wipe away the tears," as was the Indians' custom. The governor, hearing his cue, told them he would release the prisoner only if they gave up a portion of their lands.

A series of negotiations followed, the details of which were never fully recorded. Evidence suggests that the white men resorted to tactics all too common in the history of Indian relations with the U.S. government: the governor doled out more than $2,000 in cash and presents in the course of the talks, and a witness said that the money "was spent by them in the grogshops of St. Louis." When the meeting was over, the Sac delegation had signed a treaty ceding to the United States all of their territory east of the Mississippi, as well as a portion of what they claimed further west, in exchange for an annuity, or yearly payment, of $6,000 for the Sacs and $4,000 for the Foxes. With this purchase the government obtained the present state of Illinois north and west of the Illinois River, together with small sections of Wisconsin and Missouri. Harrison also wrote to the president for permission to pardon the captive warrior, but before the request could be granted, the prisoner broke free, and a soldier outside the prison cell gunned him down.

When the chiefs returned to Saukenuk, Black Hawk noticed that "they appeared to be dressed in fine coats, and had medals"—the Indians, encouraged, awaited news of their success. Quashquame, the leader of the party, reluctantly told his people of the treaty, explaining that "the American chief told them he wanted land—and they had agreed to give him some on the west side of the Mississippi, and some on the Illinois side." According to Quashquame, the chiefs "had been drunk the greater part of the time they were in St. Louis."

The Sac and Fox people could not at this point have

grasped the full meaning of the Treaty of 1804. No one had authorized Quashquame or any of the other five chiefs to give up any of their lands—they had held no council to discuss the matter, and it was not the chiefs' place to decide for them. The Sac and Fox people assumed that in St. Louis, what the chiefs had offered the whites was the use of some of their hunting grounds—a gesture of appeasement appropriate to the wrongs the war party had committed. The Sac chiefs themselves could not have understood the magnitude of their error when they placed their marks on the governor's paper—nor could they have imagined the many hardships that would follow.

An article of the treaty permitted the Sacs to remain on their territory until the U.S. government began selling the property. For the Indians, this seemed at first to mean that life could go on more or less as it had before the Cuivre River incident occurred. Gradually, however, as they watched more settlers filter into their lands—though at this point still without government sanction—the significance of the Treaty of 1804 began to sink in.

In the summer of 1805, some 150 Sacs and Foxes traveled to St. Louis to protest the incursions. General James Wilkinson, the new governor of the Louisiana Territory, was at that time helping Harrison arrange for an intertribal delegation of chiefs from his region to visit Washington, D.C. The governors hoped the trip, approved by President Thomas Jefferson, would improve relations between the United States and the Louisiana Indians. Understanding that they were on "very delicate standing" with the Sac and Fox nation, they allowed chiefs from these tribes to make up about a third of the 26-man party sent on the tour. The group, traveling by horse, boat, and carriage, arrived safely in Washington, where the president, hoping to calm the situation on the frontier, told them: "Our nation is numerous and strong; but we wish

to be just to all; and particularly to be kind and useful to all our red children."

By the time the delegation returned, however, hostilities had broken out between settlers and the Sac and Fox tribes. In November, a group of Sacs encountered some white men hunting along a branch of the Missouri River and killed two of them. Settlers accused the Indians of further attacks in the region, and the Sacs reported similar assaults on their own people. In 1806 a U.S. army officer, sent to survey the area near their villages, found the Sacs "in extreme discontent" over the Treaty of 1804, which they said was the work of "a few contemptible fellows."

The officer's mission, as it turned out, had been to find a likely spot for a U.S. fort; Wilkinson had decided to try to quiet the resentful Indians through a show of force. In 1808, the army began erecting Fort Madison on the

A party of white travelers set up camp on the banks of the Missouri River. Even before the U.S. government had authorized them to do so, settlers began filtering into Sac and Fox hunting grounds on both sides of the Mississippi.

Mississipi River, about 15 miles north of the mouth of the Des Moines River. In addition to its military function, the fort was to house a government trader, or factor, in keeping with President Jefferson's plan to offer all the tribes in the West a place to obtain supplies at a fair price. But to the Sacs, Wilkinson's main purpose was clear. Black Hawk visited the site during construction, and later wrote:

> The soldiers were busily engaged in cutting timber; and I observed that they took their arms with them, when they went to the woods—and the whole party acted as they would do in an enemy's country. . . . We could not believe that all these buildings were intended merely for the accommodation of a trader!

Soon a large party of warriors had assembled around the fort, set on discovering the soldiers' aims. As the Indians approached the gate, however,

> the soldiers, with their arms in their hands, rushed out of their rooms, where they had been concealed—the cannon was hauled in front of the gateway—and a soldier came running with fire in his hand, ready to apply the match.

At this the Sacs retreated, hardly convinced of the whites' peaceful intentions.

Meanwhile, the Sacs and Foxes continued to trade with the British, who, much to the aggravation of U.S. officials,

This French engraving depicts a mainstay of the Sac and Fox economy: the beaver. In Black Hawk's day, the beaver pelt was considered to be the world's most valuable fur. The Sac and Fox Indians continued to expand their role in the fur trade even as the issue of white settlement grew more pressing.

Shawnee leader Tecumseh raises a tomahawk in a highly romanticized 19th-century portrait. Tecumseh sought to build a united Indian front and systematically drive the whites from North America.

helped keep them suspicious of the American government. On their frequent visits to the British posts at Malden and Amherstburg, Ontario, the Indians received personal gifts—including guns and ammunition—in addition to the goods they acquired through trade. The British suppliers apparently felt they needed leverage; little by little, American traders were starting to compete with them for the Indians' business. The Indians, for their part, thought it best to expand their trade relations to include both parties, and soon they were delivering their furs to U.S. traders as well. In 1806, the American explorers Meriwether Lewis and William Clark estimated that the Sacs and Foxes—thought to be the best hunters on the Mississippi and Missouri—brought American traders $10,000 worth of furs per year.

Yet the Indians' doubts continued to mount. In 1810, the Shawnee leader Tecumseh appealed to Black Hawk to join his confederacy—an intertribal alliance the leader hoped would overpower U.S. forces and restore the Indians' supremacy throughout North America. Inspired, Black Hawk traveled with a party of Sacs to meet Tecumseh's brother, known as the Shawnee Prophet, on the Wabash River. Black Hawk recalled the prophet's words:

> He explained to us the bad treatment the different nations of Indians had received from the Americans, by giving them a few presents, and taking their land from them. I remember well his saying,— *"If you do not join your friends on the Wabash, the Americans will take this very village from you!"*

Though the Shawnee's speech impressed him, Black Hawk did not fully trust Tecumseh, and he never gave him his complete support. After Tecumseh's early campaigns against the U.S. Army proved successful, however, Black Hawk and other Sac warriors joined the Winnebagos in a series of attacks on Fort Madison. The Indians first shot flaming arrows at the fort, then bombarded it with bullets, but it was well protected and withstood the assault. Having exhausted their ammunition, the Indians returned to their villages empty-handed. In November 1811, the Sacs and Foxes learned of the Battle of Tippecanoe, in which Tecumseh's brother and his men had been decisively beaten. Many Indian nations regarded this defeat as a great setback, but Black Hawk preferred to fight his own battles, and he may have sensed that his had just begun.

5

FIGHTING THE BIG KNIVES

As Tecumseh and his brother inspired rebellion along the frontier, relations between the United States and Great Britain steadily deteriorated. Behind the antagonism between the two powers lay, among many other disputes, British and U.S. competition for the Indians' favor. In general, the Sacs preferred to deal with British traders, who offered them a better price for their furs. And the British had another important point in their favor: they offered the Indians credit. The Sacs and their British trading partners had developed a system whereby the Indians could obtain supplies—including hunting and trapping equipment—before they embarked on their winter hunt, and then return when they had furs to pay for them. The Indians had grown used to this cycle of credit and payment, and in the leaner seasons, they had come to depend on it for their survival. At this point, most American traders did not extend credit, and the Sacs avoided them accordingly.

Fearing that trade between the British and the Sacs and Foxes would lead to a military alliance, the U.S. government soon outlawed the importation of British goods. The act raised further tensions even as it failed to change the Indians' trading habits.

A Sac warrior brandishes his lance. Sac and Fox fighting power became an important asset to the British during the War of 1812.

55

The Indians' show of military strength at Tippecanoe seemed to confirm the nation's fears. Clearly, U.S. leaders thought, the British had been stirring up trouble among the Indians. In June 1812, prompted by discord on the frontier as well as commercial rivalries at sea, Great Britain and the United States went to war.

Now the contest for Indian support began in earnest. A British officer, Colonel Robert Dickson, held talks with the Sacs and Foxes and other tribes in their area, distributing presents to the Indians and otherwise arguing for their assistance in the conflict. The Americans, who may have sensed that their standing among the tribes was not high, hoped the Indians would at least remain neutral. In the summer of 1812, as a gesture of friendship, President James Madison invited a delegation of Sac chiefs to Washington, D.C. Arriving shortly after war was declared, the group received a warm welcome from the president, who told them: "I say to you, my children, your father does not ask you to join his warriors. Sit still on your seats and be witnesses that they are able to beat their enemies and protect their red friends."

Black Hawk did not take part in the trip to Washington but heard the delegates' report when they returned. According to the chiefs, the president had treated them kindly and asked the Indians not to interfere with the Americans' war. He had told them that British traders would no longer be allowed to travel the Mississippi, but that the Sacs would always be able to obtain goods from the American trader at Fort Madison. When the chiefs had reminded the president of their need for credit, he had promised that the American trader would deal with him as their British friends had done.

Black Hawk remained skeptical. He later recalled:

> I had not made up my mind whether to join the British or remain neutral. *I had not discovered one good trait in*

the character of the Americans that had come to the country! They made fair promises but never fulfilled them! Whilst the British made few—but we could always rely upon their word!

Yet most of the Sacs and Foxes thought it better to comply with American requests than to risk retaliation, and the tribe agreed to remain at peace.

The president's honor was soon tested. When the summer's corn crop had been brought in, a party of Sacs, ready to set out for the winter, made their way to Fort Madison in pursuit of supplies. "We passed merrily down the river," Black Hawk remembered, "all in high spirits. I had determined to spend the winter at my old favorite hunting ground, on Skunk river, and left part of my corn and mats at its mouth, to take up when I returned." When the Indians reached the fort, its commanding officer handed them tobacco, pipes, and other small gifts. The

Settlers travel up and down the Mississippi near Fort Madison, Iowa, in 1846. During the War of 1812, the government trader at Fort Madison was supposed to ensure that the Sacs and Foxes would not have to turn to the British for supplies.

trader, however, could offer them nothing. He had plenty of goods, he said, but had received no instructions to extend the Indians credit, and they could have no supplies without payment. "The news run through our camp like *fire in the prairie,*" Black Hawk later said. "Here ended all hopes of our remaining at peace—having been *forced into* WAR *by being* DECEIVED!"

The Indians returned to Saukenuk to find a British trader awaiting them with two boatloads of goods. Saying he had been sent by Robert Dickson, the trader presented them with a British flag, a keg of rum, and a liberal offer of credit. Black Hawk, gratified by the trader's attentions, agreed at his request to muster an army of 200 warriors and lead them to Green Bay, where Dickson would arm them for combat.

In the fall of 1812, the war chief and his men arrived at the British post, where Dickson, having already assembled a large party of Indian allies, greeted him heartily. The next day, the colonel received Black Hawk in his tent along with chiefs from the Potawatomi, Kickapoo, Ottawa, and Winnebago tribes, and placing a medal around his neck pronounced him commander of all the warriors who had gathered at Green Bay to aid the British. Having received a supply of arms, ammunition, and clothing, the Sacs joined with other warriors to form a party of 500. Under Black Hawk's command, the unit marched to Detroit, where they joined British troops and additional Indian forces fighting under Tecumseh.

From there the Indian troops, led by British commander Henry Proctor, mounted a series of attacks on U.S. posts in the region. Black Hawk's warriors contributed to an important victory at the Raisin River, in which 850 Kentucky soldiers met defeat. The campaigns gave Black Hawk occasion to compare white military tactics to his own. He noted:

Instead of stealing upon each other, and taking every advantage to *kill the enemy* and *save their own people*, as we do, . . . they marched out, in open daylight, and *fight*, regardless of the number of warriors they may lose! After the battle is over, they retire to feast, and drink wine, as if nothing had happened; after which, they make a *statement in writing*, of what they have done—*each party claiming the victory!* and neither giving an account of half the number that have been killed on their own side. They all fought like braves, but would not do to *lead a war party* with us. Our maxim is, "to *kill the enemy* and *save our own men.*" Those chiefs would do to *paddle* a canoe, but not to *steer* it.

As winter approached, Black Hawk withdrew from the fighting and headed back to Saukenuk, planning to take part in the tribe's winter hunt. Once home, the leader found that important changes had taken place among his people. British and American agents had continued to vie for Sac and Fox support, pressing the Indians with bribes and threats. Meanwhile, other tribes in the area, some of them suffering attack by U.S. forces, had begun to take sides, and eventually these Indians had badgered Sac and Fox villagers with threats of their own. The Americans had finally offered to shelter those Sacs who would migrate to U.S.-protected territory west of the Mississippi. By the end of the year, several distressed Sac and Fox bands had accepted the Americans' offer and abandoned their villages.

Troubled by this unrest among his people, Black Hawk nevertheless returned to the battlefront that year. His warriors laid siege to Fort Meigs, on the Maumee River, and in August joined in an assault on nearby Fort Stephenson. Both battles proving indecisive, by fall the leader and his band had grown discouraged and were ready to return once again to their civilian life of hunting and trading.

As they soon discovered, conditions in the Sac villages had not improved. Many of the Sacs who were reluctant

William Clark, who in 1803 helped lead the historic Lewis and Clark expedition to the Pacific Northwest, became governor of Missouri Territory in 1813. Known to many Indian tribes as the Red-Headed Chief, he was appointed superintendent of Indian affairs at St. Louis in 1822.

to support the British had remained on the Mississippi, and the Americans had continued to see these bands as potential allies. In the spring and summer of 1813, Missouri governor William Clark had continued to pressure these neutral Sacs to separate from their neighbors and come under the wing of the U.S. Army. Finally, the Indians had held a council and decided that the women, children, and old men were not secure in the absence of so many of the tribe's warriors, and should be moved to safety. In September, a group of 1,500 Sacs, accompanied by several chiefs, including Quashquame, traveled first to St. Louis, then on up the Missouri to the lands where Clark had promised them refuge.

That same month, Saukenuk had seen still further changes. Sac homelands lay directly on the border between British- and U.S.-controlled territory, and Saukenuk had remained vulnerable to attack by U.S. troops as well as Indian allies of both sides. In July 1813, a band of Potawatomis had besieged Fort Madison, and the soldiers manning the post had set fire to it and retreated to the south. In September, the Sacs had noticed a large U.S. force moving toward Peoria and had begun

Keokuk, or the Watchful Fox, eventually became a prominent member of the Sac and Fox tribe, and his image has been preserved in a number of portraits. Here he appears in traditional dress before a natural landscape.

to panic—the Americans, it seemed certain, were preparing to storm Saukenuk.

Hastily the chiefs called a council, and the tribes' spokesmen—succumbing to fear in the absence of their bold war chief—decided the entire village should flee to the west side of the Mississippi. As the chiefs and warriors were preparing to leave the council house, however, a young man approached them and asked permission to speak. Keokuk, as the man was called, had been standing in the doorway listening throughout the proceedings; he was not of a rank to enter, having never killed an enemy. His request was brash, but the circumstances, too, were extraordinary, and the council agreed to hear him out. Keokuk, as the villagers later told Black Hawk, had exhorted the leaders to stay. "Would you leave our village, desert our homes, and fly, before an enemy approaches?" he had cried to the council, "Would you leave all—even the graves of our fathers, to the mercy of an enemy, without *trying to defend them?* Give me charge of your warriors; I'll defend the village, and you may sleep in safety!" With that Keokuk became a war chief—and, as it later turned out, Black Hawk's most threatening rival.

The new leader was spared the task of defending Saukenuk on this occasion; the U.S. forces had destroyed many of the Indian villages around Peoria, but left the Sacs in peace. When Black Hawk arrived in Saukenuk that fall, the villagers, though anxious, were proceeding with their lives as usual. Black Hawk accepted Keokuk's appointment and settled down to hunt, pray, and spend time with his wife and children.

The Sacs set up their winter camp at the mouth of the Iowa River, and when he was not hunting, Black Hawk visited with neighboring tribes. One of them, the Potawatomis, had recently made peace with the United States and asked the Sacs if they would do the same. Black Hawk did not commit himself, but promised not to send war parties out against the settlers. Black Hawk's band also encountered a group of Sacs who had come up from one of the neutral bands camped on the Missouri. Bearing the scalps of white men, the "neutral" Sacs declared they wanted to join the British, but Black Hawk directed them back to their settlement.

Some time after their return to Saukenuk, the Sacs saw several boats traveling up the Mississippi, bringing reinforcements to the new U.S. fort at Prairie du Chien, at the mouth of the Wisconsin River. A short while later they heard that the British had taken the fort and were hoping the Sacs would once again join them in battle.

The Indians, their spirits revived since the winter hunt, agreed to mount an ambush on the boats that had just passed by. A war party set off by canoe and soon came in sight of the American boats, one of which the wind had driven into the shallows. With a loud war whoop the Sacs pelted the boat with bullets, and Black Hawk, shooting flaming arrows, set its sail ablaze. The Indians continued their assault as soldiers, women, and children fled the flaming ship and climbed onto a boat pulled up beside it. The rescue boat slipped quickly down the river, leaving the victory to the Indians—16 Americans were killed in the attack, and 17 were wounded. Black Hawk lost only three of his warriors. The British commander at Prairie du Chien, overjoyed at the war chief's "brilliant" performance, loaded the Sacs with presents.

The American commander at St. Louis, meanwhile, promptly sent 430 troops up the Mississippi with orders to destroy the Rock River villages. This time the Sacs were braced for battle. Informed of the U.S. operation, they enlisted the aid of the Sioux, the Foxes, and the Winnebagos, along with that of the British, in order to

defend their homes. Firing from the banks of the Missouri with well-concealed artillery, the combined forces repelled the U.S. party just outside of Saukenuk.

The Sacs came away from the battle with few casualties and their loyalties firmly set. Goaded by the British, Sac warriors surrounded a team of U.S. soldiers trying to build a fort at the mouth of the Des Moines and harassed them until they left for St. Louis. Other war parties raided settlements along the Missouri frontier; 10 American scalps turned up at Prairie du Chien, with promises of more.

By the end of 1814, the British-American conflict was in decline. To ensure the Indians' loyalty to the end, the British sent word to their Native American allies that they would agree to no treaty until the citizens of the United States returned the lands they had stolen from

The U.S. fort at Prairie du Chien overlooks the mouth of the Wisconsin River. Built in the spring of 1814, the fort was taken over by the British soon after its construction; from this strategic post British officers appealed to the Sacs for further aid.

the Indians over the past 20 years. At one meeting with a British officer, Black Hawk declared: "I have fought the Big Knives, and will continue to fight them till they are off our lands. Till then my father, your Red Children can not be happy."

Yet in the spring of 1815, with the Treaty of Ghent, the War of 1812 was over. At an intertribal council, Captain A. N. Bulger of the British forces passed a beautifully decorated peace pipe among the Indians, and the Sacs accepted the news quietly. But the Indians, perhaps understandably, were not yet ready to put down their arms. When Clark invited the Sacs and Foxes to a council at Portage des Sioux, a large delegation of Foxes responded, and so, too, did many of the Sacs who had retreated to the Missouri—but the Sacs from Rock River sent only a few warriors and a single chief. The main branch of the Sacs, still mistrustful of U.S. officials and determined above all to retain their lands, did not come to terms with the United States until the following year.

Appearing in St. Louis in May 1816, Black Hawk and a delegation of chiefs and warriors met with Clark to negotiate a treaty. When the governor denied the Indians' request that he continue to allow British traders to meet with them on their lands, the Sacs protested. Clark, however, told them he "would break off the treaty and go to war" if they insisted on causing trouble. The Sacs, cowed by the maneuvers of U.S. troops nearby, soon made their marks on the Treaty of 1816. They may not have understood that in so doing they were agreeing to "unconditionally assent to, recognize, re-establish, and confirm" the Treaty of 1804.

6

▴▴▴

INTRUDERS AT ROCK RIVER

Having at last made peace with the United States, the Sacs left St. Louis hoping to return to a quiet life. They were deeply alarmed, therefore, to find that U.S. troops were constructing a new base, Fort Armstrong, just south of Saukenuk, at a place they called Rock Island. The Indians had long prized this spot for the wide variety of berries and nuts it provided and for the fish that could be found below its cliffs. They also considered it sacred. Black Hawk remembered:

> A good spirit had care of the Island. He lived in a cave in the rocks immediately under the place where the fort now stands, and has often been seen by our people. He was white, with large wings like a swan's, but ten times larger. We were particular not to make much noise in that part of the island, for fear of disturbing him. But the noise of the fort has since driven him away, and no doubt a bad spirit has taken his place.

During the 1820s, Keokuk, with the support of white officials, gradually gained influence over a large segment of the Sac and Fox nation. This portrait by Catlin emphasizes the stature he eventually attained.

Despite the Sacs' objections, Fort Armstrong remained. Thomas Forsyth, who had been active in the fur trade at Peoria, took up residence there in order to act as the Sacs' government agent.

Meanwhile, the Sacs and Foxes continued to face the threat that had haunted them ever since Black Hawk could remember: white settlers were taking their lands.

Over the next several years, the two tribes were gradually forced to abandon most of their best hunting grounds— these lands were now fenced and farmed. The tribe's hunters soon had to travel more than 200 miles to find lands that supported game adequate to their needs.

Given these conditions, some men decided not to engage in hunting expeditions as often as they had in the past. Their people then became increasingly dependent on trade goods for their survival. Despite the objections of U.S. officials, the Sacs and Foxes continued to trade with the British, making the long trip up to Canada to meet them. The Indians' actions along the Canadian border made many white Americans suspicious. Relations between the Sacs and Foxes and their white neighbors were already tense, and British interference could only make the situation worse. One U.S. Indian agent, Henry

Soon after the Sacs and Foxes put down their weapons at the close of the War of 1812, the U.S. Army built Fort Armstrong, pictured here. From this post Thomas Forsyth, a former fur trader, monitored the Indians' activities and served as their point of contact for negotiations with the U.S. government.

This engraving, commemorating an expedition to the source of the Mississippi, is based on a sketch by Henry Schoolcraft, a government agent who dealt with Indian tribes throughout the Mississippi Valley and frequently argued on their behalf.

Schoolcraft, showed sympathy for them, writing: "The causes of this increasing intercourse [with the British] are to be found not so much in any increased efforts of the British agents to alienate these bands from our government, as in the necessitous and impoverished state of the Indians." Most U.S. leaders, however, sought to sever British-Indian relations.

At the same time, Sac and Fox hunters, in their quest for better quarry, were venturing farther and farther north and west of their usual territory. By the 1820s, their expeditions were taking them onto the prairies and plains of present-day North and South Dakota, Nebraska, and Wyoming. These, unfortunately, were the hunting lands of the Sioux, and the Sacs' incursions soon led to open hostility between the two Indian nations. As Indian warriors clashed in savage combat, their struggle spread out to include the region's white settlements, and a number of whites were killed. Chaos enveloped the frontier.

The U.S. government was appalled at the intertribal violence but did nothing to treat its cause. From St. Louis, Governor Clark sent threats to the Sacs and Foxes, declaring that they were the root of the trouble, and that if they did not cease their hostilities, he would send out troops to quell their activities. The Indians did not respond.

At Rock Island, meanwhile, Forsyth was developing another strategy. Along with distributing their annuities and monitoring their actions, Forsyth's task as agent to the Sacs and Foxes was to persuade the nation to give up Saukenuk and the rest of the land that was now officially government property. It was a difficult challenge, but the agent knew that if he could win the sympathy of an

A band of Sioux Indians performs a scalp dance. As the Sacs and Foxes encroached on Sioux hunting grounds in search of better game, the two tribes entered a period of bitter conflict.

Sac and Fox leaders gather near St. Louis. A similar delegation met with Governor William Clark in June 1821, led by the cooperative war chief Keokuk.

influential tribe member, he would be well on his way to meeting it. By 1821, the agent had found his man: the ambitious new war chief Keokuk.

In June of that year, Clark summoned two of the Sacs' warriors, who had killed a Frenchman the previous year, to a meeting at St. Louis. Expecting the Indians to resist, the governor was surprised to find, a short time later, Forsyth, Keokuk, a company of Sac and Fox leaders, and the two offenders assembled at his door. Clark soon learned that Keokuk, with Forsyth's encouragement, had gathered the delegation, and he swiftly drew the friendly leader aside. Hoping to enhance the war chief's standing among the Sacs, he promised to acknowledge Keokuk's important position among the chiefs during all of their future meetings. By the end of the Indians' visit, Clark had showered them with $300 worth of gifts, including ostrich plumes, silk handkerchiefs, and, for Keokuk, a wool coat worth $21.50. When the party returned to Saukenuk, the villagers, noticing the chiefs' profits, greeted their leader with new respect; Keokuk's ascendancy was all but assured.

It was not long before Black Hawk realized what was happening. In the next few years, the Sacs and the Foxes saw white settlement advance virtually to their doorstep. The Sacs complained to their agent regularly, but both Forsyth and Clark only increased their pressure on the Indians to leave their villages and resettle in the west. Before long, Forsyth had persuaded the principal Fox chief, with whom he had always been on good terms, to move to the other side of the Mississippi within the year. With their promises of glory, the U.S. officals soon gained Keokuk's assent as well. Black Hawk remembered the moment when he became, first and foremost, the defender of his people's lands:

> [Keokuk] sent the crier through the village to inform our people that it was the wish of our Great Father that we should remove to the west side of the Mississippi. . . . The party opposed to removing, called upon me for my opinion. I gave it freely—and after questioning Quashquame about the sale of the lands, he assured me that he "never had consented to the sale of our village." I now promised this party to be their leader, and raised the standard of opposition to Keokuk, with a full determination not to leave my village.

As settlers flooded into Sac territory, Indians and whites alike began to fear for their own safety. Black Hawk himself, while hunting near his home one day, encountered three white men who accused him of killing their hogs, beating him with sticks when he denied the claim. "I was so much bruised," he wrote later, "that I could not sleep for several nights."

The U.S. government responded to the tense situation

by exerting pressure on the Sacs to sell still more of their land. In September 1823, Keokuk appealed to Clark for a trip to Washington. He had told Black Hawk that the "Great Father" might agree to take another part of their land in exchange for the area where their villages now stood, and he wanted to meet the president and argue the Sacs' cause. Keokuk's request was granted, and in June 1824, he and his wife journeyed with nine other Sac leaders to Washington. Keokuk did speak to Secretary of War John C. Calhoun, but somehow the issue of the Rock River villages never arose. Instead, the delegation ended up signing an agreement to cede an expanse of the Sacs' territory west of the Mississippi River to Des Moines. In return, the United States paid them a sum of $1,000 and promised an additional annuity of $500 for a period of 10 years. To impress upon them the power of the United States, Clark escorted the group home by way of Baltimore, Philadelphia, and New York. Keokuk, duly intimidated, decided he had taken the right course.

The news of the sale infuriated Black Hawk. It was clear to him now that the rift dividing him from Keokuk was irreparable. "There was no more friendship existing between us," he later wrote. "I looked upon him as a coward, and no brave, to abandon his village to be occupied by strangers."

As time passed, the friction that had erupted between the Sacs and the settlers continued to escalate. Some of the whites offered to trade with their Sac neighbors but—more interested in quick profits than long-term relations—did not bother to deal with the Indians fairly. Black Hawk could see that the white presence was not only forcing his people off their usual hunting grounds but also undermining their strength. One of the settlers' primary weapons, he recalled, was alcohol: "The white people brought whisky into our village, made our people

drunk, and cheated them out of their horses, guns, and traps!" According to Black Hawk, the settlers continued to abuse his people at every opportunity. The war chief remembered a number of white attacks:

> At one time, a white man beat one of our women cruelly, for pulling a few suckers of corn out of his field, to suck, when she was hungry! At another time, one of our young men was beat with clubs by two white men for opening a fence which crossed our road, to take his horse through. His shoulder blade was broken, and his body badly bruised, from which he soon after *died!*

Offenses of this kind sent waves of bitterness throughout the Sac and Fox nation, but they could not divert Keokuk from his chosen path. In 1827, Clark gave the aspiring leader a chance to confirm his loyalty to the United States. That year the Winnebagos—longtime

In 1824, a Sac and Fox delegation under Keokuk's leadership sold the U.S. government a new tract of land stretching westward to Des Moines, and white farmers soon began to occupy it. In this picture, a settler plows a plot of land in what is now the state of Iowa.

friends of the Sacs and Foxes—mounted a series of raids on the whites in their territory, and U.S. troops were sent to quiet them. When the warring tribe called on the Foxes for aid, Clark asked the U.S. commander to appeal to Keokuk, and the war chief agreed to do what he could to keep the Sacs and Foxes on the side of the army. Keokuk not only kept his warriors from abetting the Winnebagos but persuaded them to spy for their American enemies. When the conflict was over, Clark rewarded the war chief with a saddle and bridle.

Soon after the Winnebago uprising, U.S. leaders decided it was time to act; settlers could put up with the Indian presence no longer. The governor of Illinois wrote to the secretary of war, then to Clark in St. Louis, declaring that if further bloodshed was to be avoided, the federal government needed to move all the tribes to the west side of the Mississippi, and in short order. Clark promised to have the Indians removed by May 25, 1829.

In May 1828, Forsyth called a council at Saukenuk and told the Sac and Fox chiefs that they would have to leave their villages by the following spring, regardless of their wishes. With this order, the agent set in motion a series of events that would change the lives of Black Hawk and the Sac and Fox people forever.

Lehman & Duval Lithrs

7

THE BLACK HAWK WAR

Forsyth's threats had no effect; Black Hawk and his followers refused to acknowledge the government order. As they had told the agent many times before, they would not leave the land where the bones of their ancestors lay buried, and no one—not even a U.S. war chief—could make them change their minds.

Black Hawk defended his position forcefully, but he knew it was not secure. He knew that Keokuk would obey the white man's orders, and that when Keokuk left he would take a part of the tribe with him. Black Hawk bitterly described the deep gulf between the young war chief's position and his own:

> We were a divided people, forming two parties. Keokuk being at the head of one, willing to barter our rights merely for the good opinion of the whites; and cowardly enough to desert our village to them. I was at the head of the other party, and was determined to hold on to my village, although I had been ordered to leave it. . . . It was here that I was born—and here lie the bones of many friends and relations. For this spot I felt a sacred reverence, and never could consent to leave it, without being forced therefrom.

Black Hawk was 61 years old when Thomas Forsyth first ordered the Sacs to leave Saukenuk, and he had lost none of his conviction. He was determined to fight for the land that had nourished his people for generations.

Discord troubled Saukenuk throughout the summer. Black Hawk, already anxious, noticed with anger that his rival was recruiting followers. "Keokuk," he wrote, "who has a smooth tongue, and is a great speaker, was busy in

persuading my band that I was wrong—and thereby
making many of them dissatisfied with me." By the end
of the season, many of Black Hawk's supporters had left
him.

Shortly after the Sacs left the Rock River villages for
their winter hunt, Black Hawk heard alarming rumors:
three families of whites had come to Saukenuk, destroyed
some of the Indians' lodges, and put fences through the
town, claiming the cornfields for their own use. The war
chief, 10 days' journey away, hurried back to his home,
and found that the story was true. He remembered his
shock at finding the village invaded:

> I went to my lodge and saw a family occupying it. I wished
> to talk with them, but they could not understand me. I
> then went to Rock Island, and (the agent being absent),
> told the interpreter what I wanted to say to those people,
> viz.: "Not to settle on our lands—nor trouble our lodges or
> fences—that there was plenty of land in the country for
> them to settle upon—and they must leave our village, as
> we were coming back to it in the spring." The interpreter
> wrote me a paper, and I went back to the village, and
> showed it to the intruders, but could not understand their
> reply.

Black Hawk eventually returned to the winter camp
and told his people what he had found. Alarmed, the civil
chiefs called a council, and under Keokuk's influence they
decided that it was time to comply with the white leaders'
demands. The tribe would not return to Saukenuk, they
agreed, but would set up a new village on the Iowa River
west of the Mississippi. Black Hawk saw that he had lost
the support of most of his people, but he refused to submit
to Keokuk's authority. In the spring, as the larger part of
the tribe left for their new home, he gathered what
followers he could and led them back to Saukenuk.
Keokuk accompanied them, but only, according to Black
Hawk, "to persuade others to follow him to the Ioway."

This painting, completed in 1844 by J. C. Wild, shows a village in the Iowa River valley. Most of the Sacs and Foxes moved to this area when white families began occupying Saukenuk.

The settlers had not stirred from the village, and the Indians, not knowing what else to do, resolved to take up residence among them. The two groups struggled through a summer of near constant strife. The Sacs seized the small patches of land the whites had left and planted a meager corn crop. A resentful settler refused to restrain his cattle, and the Indians' fields were overrun. One Sac protested when a white man plowed up his family's newly cultivated plot, and the settler beat him with a bean pole.

Throughout the ordeal, Black Hawk complained vigorously to Forsyth, demanding the removal of the settlers from the Sacs' homes and fields. In fact the agent sympathized, writing to Clark, "It appears hard to me that the Indian property should be stolen, their huts torn and burned down, and their persons insulted by Strangers . . . who are now quarreling and fighting with each other about the corn fields." Yet Forsyth, at this point, could do nothing.

The deadline for the Indians' departure had passed, and government officials renewed the order for removal. The United States now took its possession in hand: in July 1829, the General Land Office announced that the land around Saukenuk would go up for public sale at Springfield, Illinois, in October. The sale was also to include a portion of the Sacs' land west of the Mississippi.

Before Black Hawk and his band left for their winter hunt, Forsyth informed the war chief of the sale. The news could not dissuade the leader from his plan to return the following spring. Over the winter, Black Hawk's people obtained news of the settlement on the Iowa River; the women there had found the prairie soil difficult to work, and their harvest had been small. In Saukenuk provisions were no better, but a group from Keokuk's band nevertheless elected to leave the new village and follow Black Hawk back to their old home.

Thus augmented, Black Hawk's party spent another tense summer among the white settlers at Saukenuk. Only a small portion of the land had been sold, and the Indians occupied the area that still belonged to the government. Once again the war chief argued with Forsyth, who in turn tried to impress on the leader the urgency of the government's call for his departure. Black Hawk would not budge. This, it turned out, was to be his last debate with Forsyth—in August, after a dispute with Clark, the agent was discharged and replaced by a less experienced man, Felix St. Vrain.

Black Hawk spent a part of that season traveling, seeking advice from his Indian and British allies. A number of leaders encouraged him to defend his cause, and after a scanty harvest he told St. Vrain that his people would return in the spring of 1831, as they had in the years before.

By this time, U.S. officials had heard all they could take of the settlers' complaints; they were ready to crack down. During the winter, John Reynolds, the newly appointed governor of Illinois, appealed to the federal government for action. Clark, too, wrote to Washington. Unless the tribe could be bribed away from the region by a promise of larger annuities, he told the secretary of war, they would have to be moved by force. Settlers in the area, sensing that tensions were mounting, grew steadily more fearful of a large-scale conflict between the Sacs and the U.S. Army.

From his winter camp, Black Hawk was making preparations of his own. He sent messengers to several of the southern tribes—including his former enemies the Osages and the Cherokees—asking if they would help him defend his village against the Americans. Though these tribes remained reluctant, the war chief did receive promises of aid from the Kickapoos, Potawatomis, and some of the Winnebagos in the north. Black Hawk had found a good friend in one Winnebago leader, a mystic named White Cloud. The Winnebago Prophet, as he was sometimes known, was fiercely opposed to the Americans, and he told the Sac he would support him if he went to war.

In 1831, as he had promised, Black Hawk led a group of nearly 500 Sac men, women, and children back to their familiar lodges and fields. Eventually the season took its usual course, and clashes between the settlers and the Sacs erupted once again.

Reynolds—who considered Indians incapable of civilized behavior in any case—quickly lost patience. Calling the Sacs' return to Saukenuk an "invasion of the United States," he summoned 700 members of the Illinois militia

and gave them instructions to remove the Indians "dead or alive."

On learning of the governor's intentions, Clark alerted General Edmund P. Gaines, commander of the army's Western Department in St. Louis. The general immediately led troops to Rock Island. If he could persuade the Sacs to leave through reason and a modest show of force, Gaines thought, perhaps he could avert disaster. It was with this goal in mind that on June 5, 1831, he entered the Saukenuk council house and reminded Black Hawk and other Sac leaders that with the treaties of 1804 and 1816 they had signed their land away.

When Black Hawk had confronted the general and the council had dispersed, the Sacs withdrew for a night of restless consultation. Keokuk, who had again come to Saukenuk to exert his influence where he could, camped with his party under a large white flag. That night the smooth-tongued leader spread warnings of American

Black Hawk (left) confers with the Winnebago Prophet in an 1833 painting by Catlin.

reprisal among the members of Black Hawk's band, and nearly 50 families, fearing for their lives, decided to give up the fight and move over to his faction. When Gaines heard of Keokuk's actions, he decided to postpone the order of expulsion. He hoped the cooperative Keokuk would continue to weaken Black Hawk's forces.

Gaines soon found another good reason to hold off: reports reached him of Black Hawk's support among the other Illinois tribes. The general was particularly annoyed to hear of interference from White Cloud, whom he regarded as a schemer. Calling for Reynolds to increase his forces, he delayed his attack further until the militia could arrive.

On June 25, 1831, 1,400 volunteers arrived at Rock Island, bearing, according to Gaines, "an excess of the *Indian ill-will,* so that it required much gentle persuasion to restrain them from killing, indiscriminately, all the Indians they met."

The angry troops stormed Saukenuk—but the Sacs were nowhere to be found. Black Hawk and his people had escaped across the Mississippi during the night. Furious, the soldiers demolished what property they could lay their hands on, then burned the entire village to the ground.

Black Hawk, camped a short distance away, realized that without the aid his allies had promised him he could not stop the white men. When Gaines called him to another council, therefore, the war chief agreed to meet him. On June 30, Black Hawk and some of his warriors appeared before the general and placed their marks on another paper. Titled "Articles of Agreement and Capitulation," the document committed the Sacs to breaking all ties with the British, accepting Keokuk as their principal authority, and allowing the United States to build roads across their lands in Iowa. In a gesture of peace, Gaines promised that the settlers of Rock River would assist the displaced Sacs with a year's supply of corn.

Black Hawk, insulted as he was by the promotion of

A Fox warrior holds a war club studded with brass nails. The Foxes went to battle against the Menominees in 1831, frightening the settlers near them until the government intervened.

Keokuk, might have accepted these terms, but Gaines's offer of aid did not take shape as he expected. The militia, who felt the general had been too soft, disparaged the "corn treaty" and harassed the fugitive Sacs with gunfire as soon as Gaines and his troops were gone. Finding the militia on their side, the settlers ignored Gaines's instructions, parceling out to the Indians only a small ration of corn. The Sacs, destitute in their makeshift camps, started to send small parties across the river to harvest the fields that had once been theirs. The settlers drove them away with gunshot.

Elsewhere, another storm was brewing. The previous year, a band of Sioux and Menominee warriors had attacked a Fox settlement, killing some of its chiefs. Fox custom demanded that the score be evened, and in July 1831, while Black Hawk's people faced starvation, the Foxes raided the Menominees, killing 28 of their people. The settlers of the region, who feared the violence would spread, demanded that the Fox offenders be arrested and tried for murder. The Foxes soon found federal authorities at their door and, at a loss, sent a runner to Black Hawk, requesting his advice. The news angered the war chief, who saw no reason for the whites to bother with intertribal affairs. He told the Foxes to stand their ground.

At about this time, one of Black Hawk's warriors, an aggressive 30-year-old named Neapope, returned from Canada, having left for that country when Gaines's troops first approached Saukenuk. Neapope told the war chief that he had spoken with the British, and that they had defended the Sacs' claim to the Rock River area and promised to send guns, ammunition, and provisions should the Sacs and Foxes go to war. Neapope had also stopped at White Cloud's town, he said, and the prophet had assured him that the Sacs could count on his own band, as well as the Potawatomis, Chippewas, and Ottawas, if they ever needed more warriors.

Believing now that he still had a battle to fight and the means to fight it with, Black Hawk proclaimed to his band that they would reclaim Saukenuk the following year. By the spring of 1832, despite Keokuk's words of protest, Black Hawk had recruited some 600 warriors and their families, including a large contingent of Foxes— who had joined him in response to his encouragement the previous summer—as well as Kickapoos, Winnebagos, and Potawatomis. Keokuk, finding his authority thwarted, sent a message to St. Vrain at Rock Island, warning him of the impending invasion.

The Black Hawk War had begun. General Henry

Atkinson, commander of U.S. troops in the region, led a force of more than 200 soldiers to Rock Island, hoping to prevent Black Hawk's followers from crossing to the east side of the Mississippi. By the time the troops reached Fort Armstrong, however, Black Hawk's group, numbering more than 2,000 in all, had crossed the river near the mouth of the Iowa and were heading north toward Saukenuk.

Some time before the Indians reached the village, White Cloud met them and warned them of the army's presence. The prophet invited Black Hawk's band to join him at his own settlement farther up the Rock River, where they could wait for help from the other tribes. Black Hawk accepted the offer, and the Indians quietly turned up the Rock River, skirted Fort Armstrong, and continued north and east until they reached the Winnebago village.

At this point Atkinson, unsure how to proceed, appealed to Reynolds for reinforcements. Announcing that Americans were in "eminent danger," the governor issued an appeal for volunteers. More than 1,700 men responded, among them 23-year-old Abraham Lincoln, at that time a store clerk in New Salem, Illinois. Reynolds's unit, burning for adventure, proceeded to Rock Island, where they met Atkinson's forces on May 7, 1832.

Black Hawk, camped with his Winnebago friends, began to receive messages from Atkinson, commanding him to bring his people back across the Mississippi. The war chief challenged the general to come and face him where he was. As time passed, however, and no allies came to join his forces, Black Hawk grew restless. White Cloud's Winnebagos, though sympathetic, showed little interest in helping the Sacs test the U.S. Army's power. The war chief decided to take his band farther north and seek aid among the Potawatomis. The group moved on,

General Henry Atkinson, who led the U.S. Army's assault on Black Hawk, posed for this portrait in 1832. The Indians called him the White Beaver.

and near present-day Rockford, Illinois, Black Hawk met with a Potawatomi deputation. But this tribe, too, disappointed him. Suspecting Neapope of deception, the war chief soon began to despair of British help as well. The Sac and Fox band by this time had almost no provisions, and Black Hawk saw that his situation was desperate. He decided to turn back.

By this time it was too late for the Indians to retreat peacefully. Atkinson, with more than 2,000 men, was marching to overtake them. The army had divided into detachments and was working its way north and east. General Samuel Whiteside, leading a unit of 1,500 mounted militiamen, descended on the prophet's village and, finding that Black Hawk had left, burned the settlement down. His men proceeded up the Rock River to Dixon's Ferry, where they waited for a supply unit to catch up with them.

Winnebago villagers gather outside their lodges. Black Hawk and his band, finding themselves outnumbered by U.S. troops, sought refuge among the Winnebagos.

Informed that Black Hawk and his followers were just 25 miles upstream, Whiteside's troops craved action. Finally, on the morning of May 14, Reynolds—who had accompanied the general as commander in chief of the militia—sent out a battalion of 275 men under Major Isaiah Stillman, with orders to pursue the band and "coerce them into submission."

When Black Hawk learned of the soldiers' approach, he was holding a ceremony with a group of Potawatomis and had no more than 50 of his warriors with him. Feeling he had no choice but to surrender, he sent three of his men to meet Stillman with a white flag of truce. Because he was not sure how the Americans would react, he asked another party of five warriors to follow the first group and take note of what happened.

The volunteers had just set up camp, and on seeing the Sacs approach they jumped to their feet in excitement. No sooner had the Americans drawn the delegation into the camp and begun to interrogate them than one of their scouts spotted a member of the second party. The white men flew into a panic, leapt onto their horses, and charged out into the prairie, thinking to forestall an Indian attack. Terrified, the five warriors turned to flee, and the volunteers began firing. As two of the Indians fell outside the camp, the three flag bearers stood at the mercy of a group of whites who guarded them suspiciously. Suddenly the settlers drew their guns and began firing. Two of the Indians escaped in the confusion; the other was shot dead.

The survivors of the second group returned to Black Hawk's camp in time to warn him of the Americans' approach. Hoping to save what lives he could, the war chief gathered 40 of his men and led them into hiding. As the horsemen rode up near them, Black Hawk gave out a yell, and his warriors rushed out firing. Some of the soldiers dropped, while others wheeled on their horses and stampeded back toward the camp. Shouting that a

Though ill prepared for combat, Black Hawk forced U.S. soldiers into retreat during the battle known as Stillman's Run.

thousand Indians were after them, they induced the entire unit to retreat to the camp at Dixon's Ferry. In the end the defeat proved modest—11 whites were killed—but it disheartened the volunteers, and all but 250 left for home.

Black Hawk, surprised at his own success, led his band north toward what is now Wisconsin. At the head of the Kishwaukee River, the Sacs were greeted by a party of Winnebagos, who guided them to the Four Lakes area of central Wisconsin. The Indians settled in for a period, concealing themselves in the marshes.

Meanwhile, word of Black Hawk's accomplishments had spread across the prairie, and bands of Potawatomis, Winnebagos, and Kickapoos began to set out on small campaigns of their own. In a well-publicized raid on a settlement at Indian Creek, a Potawatomi war band killed and mutilated 15 people; some Winnebago warriors descended south and slew the Rock Island agent St. Vrain. Soon Black Hawk himself was sending out war parties from his place of hiding, and skirmishes broke out all along the western border of Illinois and Wisconsin.

With every report of an Indian attack, the settlers' terror mounted. "The alarm and distress on the frontier cannot be described," wrote an officer at the time. "It is heart rending to see the women and children in an agony of fear, fleeing from their homes and hearths, to seek what they imagine is but a brief respite from death."

The settlers' cries of anger and fear soon reached the ears of President Andrew Jackson, a confirmed enemy of the Indians.

Already impatient with Atkinson's failings, he wrote to his war secretary: "Black Hawk and his party must be chastized and a speedy and honorable termination put to this war, which will hereafter deter others from the like unprovoked hostilities by Indians on our frontier."

By June 12, Atkinson had replenished his army with 2,000 new volunteers, and he was moving again. As he followed Black Hawk's tracks up the Rock and Kishwaukee rivers, he soon ran into swampy country, lost the trail, and ran short of supplies, at which point his progress ended. His militia, hungry, sick, and plagued by mosquitoes, went home at the end of their enlistments.

By now Black Hawk's people were themselves near starvation, subsisting on roots, grasses, and bark from trees. Knowing they had to move on, the war chief decided to try to bring the band to the Sac settlements along the Iowa. There, he thought, the Americans might leave them in peace. Still hopeful, Black Hawk and his followers set out west, but before they could travel far, calamity struck.

Colonel Henry Dodge, commander of a unit of volunteers, had obtained news of Black Hawk's position from a group of Winnebago informers. From Black Hawk's camp in the Four Lakes district, Dodge and his men picked up the Indians' trail. They soon reached a hill overlooking the Wisconsin River, and a scouting party spied the band crossing to an island in the center of the river. Dodge's army quickly descended on the weary Sacs.

Stealing up a nearby hill and firing down on the white men, Black Hawk and his warriors held them off while the rest of their people tried to paddle across to safety. The troops eventually drove the warriors back and into a ravine where they were sheltered by tall grasses. From there the Indians held their ground until nightfall, when the fire dropped off and they were able to join their families across the river.

By the time the battle was over, the Americans had suffered only one casualty. According to Black Hawk, six of his men were killed; Dodge estimated the Indians' losses at 40. Weak and battered, the Sacs left the Wisconsin and continued west across country. It was an arduous journey. Most of the wounded grew steadily worse and perished along the way; other Indians sickened and died of starvation. Abandoning possessions with every step, the Sacs left a trail of traps, kettles, blankets, and other belongings as they staggered forward. By August 1, the slow and painful trek had brought the band to the mouth of the Bad Axe River, about 40 miles north of Prairie du Chien.

Having at last reached the Mississippi, the Indians assembled rough canoes and rafts from the materials around them and set out to cross the river. They had not gone far when a huge steamboat came into view. Bearing the name *Warrior*, the boat was on its way south from a mission in Minnesota, and it carried a detachment of troops and a six-pound piece of artillery. Black Hawk, who knew the boat's captain, immediately raised a white flag and sent one of his men to tell the commander that the Sacs were ready to surrender. The message was misinterpreted, and after a confused exchange the Americans opened fire. At least 23 Indians were killed in the sudden onslaught; the rest took cover in the trees and returned the soldiers' fire. After a battle of about two hours, the *Warrior* retreated south for fuel.

At this point Black Hawk took a small party north to seek help among the Chippewas, leaving his people to proceed as they thought best. A runner soon overtook his party with ominous news: The Sacs were again making their way across the river, and many had already arrived safely on the western shore. But the white army was moving swiftly toward them and was now only a few miles away.

Encouraged by what he learned from Dodge, Atkinson had renewed his forces and followed Black Hawk's path across the Wisconsin prairie. On August 3, 1832, he and his 1,300-man regiment reached the Mississippi where the Sacs were attempting to cross.

Black Hawk did not appear in time to fight for the lives of his people. "They tried to give themselves up," one of his warriors later told him. "The whites paid no attention to their entreaties—but commenced *slaughtering* them!" Indeed, Atkinson's troops pounded the fleeing Sacs with bullets, ignoring their helpless condition. Groups of warriors tried to defend their families; wielding clubs and rifles, the white men cut them down. Some Indians tried to swim the river, the women carrying their children on their backs; these were, according to an American witness, "coolly picked off by sharp-shooters, who exercised no more mercy towards squaws and children than they did towards braves—treating them all as though they were rats instead of human beings." At the height of the battle the *Warrior* reappeared, and the boat's six-pounder blasted more of the Indians out of the woods where they were hiding. The massacre continued for eight full hours. When it was over, at least 150 Indians lay dead, and 39 had been taken prisoner. Those who escaped across the river quickly fell into the hands of the Sioux, who killed and scalped 68 of them, sparing only 22 women and children.

Numb with sorrow, Black Hawk and his remaining

followers pushed north toward the country of the Winnebagos. Their war was over, and their retreat did not last long. Shortly after they reached the Wisconsin Dells, a Winnebago band overtook the party—the government, it turned out, was offering $100 in cash and 20 ponies for Black Hawk's capture. The war chief gave up without a fight. According to his autobiography, he quietly turned to a chief among the Winnebagos and handed the man his sacred bundle. He assured the chief that the medicine bag—"the soul of the Sac nation"—had never been dishonored in battle. "Take it," he said. "It is my life—dearer than life." Then, accompanied by his two sons and the Winnebago Prophet, he followed his captors to Prairie du Chien and on August 27, 1832, surrendered to the government agent.

From Prairie du Chien, Black Hawk and his companions were sent to Fort Crawford, where they remained for a time under the custody of future U.S. president Zachary Taylor. Taylor in turn sent them by boat down the Mississippi to Jefferson Barracks. The trip, Black Hawk later remembered, was a time of sad reflection:

> On our way down, I surveyed the country that had cost us so much trouble, anxiety, and blood, and that now caused me to be a prisoner of war. I reflected upon the ingratitude of the whites, when I saw their fine houses, rich harvests, and every thing desirable around them; and recollected that all this land had been ours, . . . and that the whites were not satisfied until they took our village and our grave-yards from us, and removed us across the Mississippi.

Black Hawk had waged a valiant struggle on behalf of his people, but the United States, determined to push its boundary westward, had defeated him.

8

THE GREAT FOG

Soon after Black Hawk's surrender, Reynolds met with Keokuk and some of the other leaders from the villages along the Iowa. "The power to dictate terms," the governor noted at the time, "is very much in our hands." Reynolds first pronounced Keokuk head chief of the Sac and Fox nation, then pressured the Indians until they agreed to cede a strip of land 60 miles wide along the Mississippi River in the present state of Iowa, promising never again to "reside, plant, fish, or hunt, on any portion of the ceded land." In exchange for the tract, which encompassed some 6 million acres, the Sacs and Foxes were promised an annuity of $2,000 for a period of 30 years. Their total compensation, $60,000, fell far short of what the land was worth: according to estimates at the time, more than $7 million.

Black Hawk and the other prisoners remained at Jefferson Barracks, under Atkinson's command, throughout the fall and winter. To his utter humiliation, the war chief was forced to wear a ball and chain. The restriction

Black Hawk's oldest son, Nasheaskuk, or Whirling Thunder, surrendered to government authorities along with his father. During his imprisonment he posed for this portrait by Catlin.

95

was unnecessary—Black Hawk's surrender had been genuine, and to escape at this point would have been to him an act of dishonor.

In the spring of 1833, Black Hawk's wife and daughter visited him at Jefferson Barracks. At the same time, a group of Sac leaders, including Keokuk—who, in his new position, may have felt that it was time to put rivalries aside—petitioned Atkinson for the war chief's release. Before he could return to his people, however, officials insisted that he and his companions, as prisoners of the United States, spend time at Fort Monroe, near the nation's capital.

Traveling by boat and by carriage, the group reached Washington late in April and was immediately taken to

Black Hawk and five other Sac and Fox prisoners, restricted by ball and chain, await their release at Jefferson Barracks.

meet with President Jackson. The "Great White Father" treated the prisoners politely, but demanded to know why Black Hawk had fought against the United States. "I thought he ought to have known this before," the war chief later wrote, "and, consequently, said but little to him about it—as I expected he knew as well as I could tell him" A guard soon delivered the Indians to Fort Monroe. There, uncertain of their future, they waited.

Finally, in June 1833, the president ordered Black Hawk's release. Jackson saw to it that the old war chief and his group, like Keokuk before them, traveled back west by way of some of the nation's largest cities.

Passing through Norfolk, Baltimore, Philadelphia, New York, and Albany, Black Hawk had an effect on the American public that Jackson had not expected. Newspapers had spread the story of the Black Hawk War, as the conflict had been termed, all over the nation, and in the East, many citizens sympathized with the Indians' plight. Other fans were less enlightened—this was simply their chance to see a "dangerous savage" face to face. In keeping with the president's plan, the group met with mayors and other civic officials and toured shipyards, railroads, markets, and government arsenals filled with arms. But Black Hawk also became guest of honor at numerous banquets, received gifts, and attracted enormous crowds wherever he went, outshining Jackson, who was on a public speaking tour at the time. At the Norfolk Navy Yard, Black Hawk inspected the 74-gun ship *Delaware*; in Philadelphia he went to the theater; in New York he watched a balloonist take to the sky and nodded politely as an admirer presented him with a pair of earrings to take to his wife.

Newspapers kept a careful account of Black Hawk's activities and underscored his enthusiastic reception. Along with other admirers, a reporter from *Niles' Weekly*

Register was especially impressed with Black Hawk's eldest son, Nasheaskuk. He wrote:

> Had his countenance not been wanting in that peculiar expression which emanates from a cultivated intellect and which education alone can give, we could have looked upon him as the living personification of our "beau ideal" of manly beauty.

Having traveled on through Buffalo, the Great Lakes region, and Detroit, Black Hawk arrived in Iowa deeply impressed by the power of the United States and the generosity of its people. Thinking back on the journey later, he wrote:

A steamboat carries passengers past Detroit. On the journey west from Washington, Black Hawk's party made stops at some of the nation's major cities, ending with the western outposts along the Great Lakes.

> I feel grateful to the whites for the kind manner they
> treated me and my party, whilst travelling among them—
> and from my heart I assure them, that the whites will al-
> ways be welcome in our village or camps. We will forget
> what has past—and may the watchword between Ameri-
> cans and Sacs ever be Friendship! May the Great Spirit
> keep our people and the whites always at peace.

In August 1833, Black Hawk finally came to the
Mississippi River and began the last part of his journey
home. Although he was glad of the signs of friendship
he had seen in the East, he was also cautious about the
future. As he traveled south, he was surprised to see that
settlers had already built sizable towns on the west side
of the Mississippi. Black Hawk told his interpreter

> I have since found the country much settled by the whites
> near to our people. . . . I am very much afraid, that in a
> few years, they will begin to drive and abuse our people, as
> they have formerly done. I may not live to see it, but I feel
> certain that the day is not distant.

At Prairie du Chien, Major John Garland, who had
accompanied the Indians on the tour, released White
Cloud to the Winnebagos. The Sac party traveled on to
Rock Island, where Garland called another meeting of
Sac and Fox leaders. The commander opened the meeting
with a message from Jackson directing Black Hawk to
follow the leadership of his old rival Keokuk. Black Hawk,
beside himself with humiliation, gave one final cry of
protest. Minutes later, his pride vanquished, he apologized
for his outburst and dutifully accepted the injunction.
Stripped of his authority by white officials and humbled
by the might of the American nation, the war chief would
never again raise his voice against the U.S. government.

It was at this time that Black Hawk asked the
interpreter Antoine LeClaire to record his story so that
his own view of the Sac and Fox struggle might be
preserved. Soon after LeClaire took down the narrative,

a newspaperman, John B. Patterson, revised the manuscript and had it published. *Life of Black Hawk* remains one of the most accurate and complete records historians possess of a Native American's thoughts and emotions during the period of Indian removal.

Black Hawk and his sons eventually joined the rest of their family in Iowa Territory, and together they set up a small house near the Des Moines River. Like other members of the Sac and Fox nation, they tried to continue with the life they had known before their conflict with the whites. Black Hawk's wife planted a garden, and her daughter helped her tend it. Black Hawk continued to hunt, trade, and speak at village councils. But game was scarce, and the Sacs and Foxes never returned to the prosperity of former times.

Throughout the 1830s, settlers continued their expansion westward. White-populated towns soon sprang up near Sac and Fox territory, and the old troubles returned. Discouraged by the paltry profits their hunting brought them, some Indians began spending their winters hovering around the white settlements. The tribes' annuities allowed them to pay for the American goods they wanted, but the close contact with the whites soon proved disastrous. Large numbers of Sacs and Foxes, who had no immunities to the diseases that the whites had brought from Europe, quickly fell victim to influenza, smallpox, and measles. The Sac and Fox population, numbering approximately 6,000 in 1833, by 1846 was reduced to around 1,200. White traders also continued to supply the tribes with alcohol and to cheat them in their transactions. John Beach, agent to the Sacs and Foxes during this period, declared that except during hunting expeditions far from the whites, the Indians' villages presented a "continual scene of the most revolting intoxication." The

Indians grew more and more dependent on credit, and poverty became widespread.

At the same time, the U.S. government began to pressure Sac and Fox leaders to cede even more of their territory. In September 1836, at Keokuk's suggestion, a party of Sac chiefs met with U.S. officials and agreed to cede 400 square miles of their reservation in order to pay off the debts their people had incurred. One Sac leader remarked sadly: "We are unable to end the great fog of white people which is rolling toward the setting sun." Black Hawk was present at the meeting but remained quiet.

The following year, Black Hawk and other Sac leaders traveled to Washington, D.C., to attend another treaty council. With the Treaty of 1837, the Sacs agreed to cede an additional 1.25 million acres adjacent to the tract given up the previous year, receiving in return $100,000 and a small annuity. The treaty included a further provision: the Sacs and Foxes were to allow white teachers and clergymen to enter their communities. The government soon set up schools where Sac children could be taught to speak English and adopt white ways. Protestant missionaries came to Sac and Fox villages and tried to persuade the Indians to become Christians. Although the Indians treated these newcomers kindly, few of them paid much attention to their advice.

Throughout these difficult times, Black Hawk did his best to support his people, but his fighting spirit was gone. George Catlin, an artist who spent much of his life observing the Indians and documenting their history, wrote of the war chief's appearance at the 1836 treaty council: "With an old frock coat and brown hat on, and a cane in his hand, he stood the whole time outside of the group, and in dumb and dismal silence."

Black Hawk died on October 3, 1838, at the age of 71. His body was laid to rest in the traditional Sac manner, sitting erect in a small wooden hut above ground. But Black Hawk could not find peace even in death. In 1839, a settler robbed the war chief's grave and sold his bones to the museum of the Geological and Historical Society in Burlington, Iowa. The museum was destroyed in a fire in 1855.

In their leader's absence, Black Hawk's people still struggled to survive as white settlers continued their relentless push westward. In 1842, Sac and Fox leaders signed a treaty giving up the last of their land in Iowa. The Indians received about $250,000 and agreed to move

Black Hawk's funeral is depicted in this painting by Catlin. The war chief was seated upright in a wooden hut, according to Sac custom, and left to rest in what is now northeastern Davis county, Iowa.

west of the Missouri River, along the Osage River in present-day Kansas, where they would share about 400,000 acres with members of the Ottawa, Chippewa, and Kansas tribes.

The Sacs and Foxes hoped for a new life in Kansas, but their old troubles continued. The rough prairie land of the new territory was difficult to farm; to the north, where game was more plentiful, the tribes' hunters met with hostile Indians; disease claimed more and more Sac and Fox lives. And by the 1860s, white settlers were beginning to claim land in this territory as well. In 1867, the Sacs and Foxes gave up their Kansas home and accepted another tract of land in what is now called Oklahoma.

In the years that followed, a small group returned to Kansas, bought back some of the land they had ceded, and maintained their own community among the whites. Those who stayed in Oklahoma were eventually forced to divide their land so that each family kept an allotment of only 160 acres. The land that remained was sold to white settlers.

Over the years, the Sacs and Foxes, finding the Oklahoma land unyielding, have gradually turned from farming to other work. By 1920, more than half of the tribes' families had sold their allotments. Some of these people have gone on to work as farm laborers close by; others have left the region to seek jobs in the cities of Oklahoma and elsewhere. A number of those who retained their lands have been able to lease them to oil and gas companies to supplement their income. In 1990, 4,704 Sac and Fox Indians were living on the lands they had been given in Oklahoma; 45 members of the tribe continued to live on the land they had bought in Kansas. The lives of today's Sac and Fox Indians are very different from those of their parents and grandparents. They have

A bustling village graces the banks of a river in Kansas. The government directed the Sacs to move to this area in 1842. They remained in Kansas until 1867, when white settlement forced their removal once again.

survived many hardships, and they will continue to find new ways of living—ways that combine their old customs with the many other traditions that make up American life. And, as they face the future, the Sac and Fox people can remember with pride the legacy of courage and wisdom left by their great defender, Black Hawk.

CHRONOLOGY

1767 — Born in Saukenuk, at the junction of the Mississippi and Rock rivers

1804 — Sac leaders sign first treaty with United States, ceding all land east of Mississippi River

1812–15 — Black Hawk sides with British during War of 1812

1816 — Black Hawk and other Sac leaders sign treaty with United States pledging peace and friendship, reaffirming Treaty of 1804

1824 — Keokuk and other Sacs sign treaty with United States, ceding a tract of land west of Mississippi River

1829 — Thomas Forsyth orders Sacs and Foxes to abandon lands east of the Mississippi; United States begins selling Sac and Fox land to settlers; the majority of Sacs resettle in Iowa

1831 — Edmund P. Gaines meets Black Hawk and his followers at Saukenuk and threatens removal; Illinois troops destroy Saukenuk; Black Hawk and other Sac warriors sign "Articles of Agreement and Capitulation"

Spring 1832 — Black Hawk leads supporters back to Saukenuk; they camp with the Winnebagos on Rock River; hoping to surrender, they instead defeat U.S. troops at Stillman's Run; they retreat to central Wisconsin

July 1832 — Black Hawk's followers cross Wisconsin River and are attacked by U.S. Army; 70 Indians are killed

August 1832 — More than 150 Sac and Fox men, women, and children are killed in the Battle of the Bad Axe; Black Hawk surrenders and is imprisoned at Jefferson Barracks, Missouri

September 1832 — Keokuk signs treaty with United States, ceding 6 million acres west of Mississippi River

April 1833 — Black Hawk meets with President Andrew Jackson in Washington, D.C.; Black Hawk is imprisoned in Virginia

June 1833 — Released from prison; returns to Iowa after touring cities in East and Midwest

1837 — Sacs and Foxes sign treaty with United States, ceding 1.25 million acres in Iowa

1838 — Black Hawk dies at the age of 71

1842 — Sacs and Foxes cede all land in Iowa and agree to move west into Kansas

1867 — Sacs and Foxes cede land in Kansas and agree to move to Oklahoma

FURTHER READING

Bauxar, J. Joseph. "History of the Illinois Area." In *The Northeast,* edited by B. Trigger. Vol. 15, *Handbook of North American Indians,* 594-601. Washington, D.C.: Smithsonian Institution Press, 1978.

Black Hawk. *Black Hawk: An Autobiography.* Edited by Donald Jackson. Urbana: University of Illinois Press, 1964.

Callender, Charles. "Sauk." In *The Northeast,* edited by B. Trigger. Vol. 15, *Handbook of North American Indians,* 648-55. Washington, D.C.: Smithsonian Institution Press, 1978.

Hagan, William. *The Sac and Fox Indians.* Norman: University of Oklahoma Press, 1958.

Josephy, Alvin M. "The Rivalry of Black Hawk and Keokuk." In *The Patriot Chiefs: A Chronicle of American Indian Resistance,* 210-53. *New York: Viking Press, 1958.*

INDEX

PICTURE CREDITS

Cincinnati Historical Society: pp. 45 (neg. #8-93-201), 52 (neg. #B-92-364); Courtesy of Independence National Park Collection: p. 60; Courtesy of the Illinois State Historical Library: p. 86; Kansas State Historical Society: pp. 21, 26, 71; Library of Congress: pp. 10 (neg. #LC-USZ62-86), 12 (neg. #LC-USZ62-33775), 13 (neg. #LC-USZ62-15514), 18, 30 (neg. #LC-USZ62-34017), 33 (neg. #LC-USZ62-2736), 34 (neg. #LC-USZ62-5034), 44 (neg #LC-USZ62-270), 57 (neg. #LC-USZ62-3422), 61 (neg. #LC-USZ62-32585), 68 (neg. #LC-USZ62-3417), 69 (neg. #LC-USZ62-8181), 76, 79 (neg. #LC-USZ62-3424), 84 (neg. #LC-USZ62-1197), 98 (neg. #LC-USZ62-17051), 104 (neg. #LC-USZ62-3666), 106 (neg. #LC-USZ62-01675); Paul Mellon Collection © 1993, National Gallery of Art, Washington: pp. 82 (*Black Hawk and the Profit-Saukie*), 96 (*Black Hawk and Five Other Sauki Prisoners*), 102 (*Funeral of Black Hawk-Saukie*); Missouri Historical Society, Photographs and Prints Collection: pp. 28, 38 (*Three Braves*, George Catlin), 64 (*Prairie du Chien, Wisconsin* Henry Lewis: Das Illustrirte Mississippithal); National Archives of Canada: p. 51; National Museum of American Art, Washington, D.C./Art Resource, N.Y.: pp. 2, 16, 24, 54, 66, 94; The Research Libraries, The New York Public Library, Astor, Lenox & Tilden Foundations: pp. 32, 70, 87, 89; State Historical Society of Iowa–Iowa City: p. 74; State Historical Society of North Dakota: p. 50; State Historical Society of Wisconsin: p. 42 (WHi(x3)38421).

NANCY BONVILLAIN is an adjunct professor at the New School for Social Research. She has a Ph.D. in anthropology from Columbia University. Dr. Bonvillain has written a grammar book and dictionary of the Mohawk language as well as *The Huron* (1989) and *The Mohawk* (1992) for the Chelsea House INDIANS OF NORTH AMERICA series.

W. DAVID BAIRD is the Howard A. White Professor of History at Pepperdine University in Malibu, California. He holds a Ph.D. from the University of Oklahoma and was formerly on the faculty of history at the University of Arkansas, Fayetteville, and Oklahoma State University. He has served as president of both the Western History Association, a professional organization, and Phi Alpha Theta, the international honor society for students of history. Dr. Baird is also the author of *The Quapaw Indians: A History of the Downstream People* and *Peter Pitchlynn: Chief of the Choctaws* and the editor of *A Creek Warrior of the Confederacy: The Autobiography of Chief G. W. Grayson.*